D0948184

Hold Everything Dear

Pantheon Books, New York

All rights reserved. Published in the United States by Pantheon Books,
a division of Random House, Inc., New York, and in Canada by
Random House of Canada Limited, Toronto. Originally published in
Great Britain by Verso, an imprint of New Left Books, London.

Pantheon Books and colophon are registered trademarks of
Random House, Inc.

Grateful acknowledgment is made to Gareth Evans for permission to
reprint "Hold Everything Dear" by Gareth Evans. Copyright © 2005 by
Gareth Evans. Reprinted by permission.

Library of Congress Cataloging-in-Publication Data
Berger, John.
Hold everything dear : dispatches on survival and resistance/John Berger.
        p.   cm.
Includes bibliographical references.
ISBN-13: 978-0-375-42509-7
1. Security, International.   2. War—Causes.   3. Equality.   4. Power
(Social sciences).   5. International economic relations.   6. War on
Terrorism, 2001
I. Title.
JZ5588.B467 2007   355'.033—dc22   2007012673

www.pantheonbooks.com

Printed in the United States of America
First American Edition
2   4   6   8   9   7   5   3   1

Contents

CONTENTS

After 'Guernica' (1937) — Beirut, Cana, Tyr (2006)

Hold Everything Dear

for John Berger

as the brick of the afternoon stores the rose heat of the journey

as the rose buds a green room to breathe
and blossoms like the wind

as the thinning birches whisper their silver stories of the wind to the urgent
in the trucks

as the leaves of the hedge store the light
that the moment thought it had lost

as the nest of her wrist beats like the chest of a wren in the turning air

as the chorus of the earth find their eyes in the sky
and unwrap them to each other in the teeming dark

hold everything dear

the calligraphy of birds across the morning
the million hands of the axe, the soft hand of the earth
one step ahead of time
the broken teeth of tribes and their long place

         steppe-scattered and together

clay's small, surviving handle, the near ghost of a jug
carrying itself towards us through the soil

the pledge of offered arms, the single sheet that is our common walking
the map of the palm held
in a knot

     but given as a torch

hold everything dear

the paths they make towards us and how far we open towards them

the justice of a grass that unravels palaces but shelters the songs of the searching

the vessel that names the waves, the jug of this life, as it fills with the days
as it sinks to become what it loves

memory that grows into a shape the tree always knew as a seed

the words
the bread

the child who reaches for the truths beyond the door

the yearning to begin again together
animals keen inside the parliament of the world

the people in the room the people in the street the people

hold everything dear

19th May 2005
Gareth Evans

Hold Everything Dear

Twelve Theses on the Economy of the Dead

(1994)

1. The dead surround the living. The living are the core of the dead. In this core are the dimensions of time and space. What surrounds the core is timelessness.

2. Between the core and its surroundings there are exchanges, which are not usually clear. All religions have been concerned with making them clearer. The credibility of religion depends on the clarity of certain unusual exchanges. The mystifications of religion are the result of trying to systematically produce such exchanges.

3. The rarity of clear exchange is due to the rarity of what can cross intact the frontier between timelessness and time.

4. To see the dead as the individuals they once were tends to obscure their nature. Try to consider the living as we

might assume the dead to do: collectively. The collective would accrue not only across space but also throughout time. It would include all those who have ever lived. And so we would also be thinking of the dead. The living reduce the dead to those who have lived; yet the dead already include the living in their own great collective.

5. The dead inhabit a timeless moment of construction continually rebegun. The construction is the state of the universe at any instant.

6. According to their memory of life, the dead know the moment of construction as, also, a moment of collapse. Having lived, the dead can never be inert.

7. If the dead live in a timeless moment, how can they have a memory? They remember no more than being thrown into time, as does everything which existed or exists.

8. The difference between the dead and the unborn is that the dead have this memory. As the number of dead increases, the memory enlarges.

9. The memory of the dead existing in timelessness may be thought of as a form of imagination concerning the possible. This imagination is close to (resides in) God; but I do not know how.

10. In the world of the living there is an equivalent but contrary phenomenon. The living sometimes experience timelessness, as revealed in sleep, ecstasy, instants of extreme danger, orgasm, and perhaps in the experience of dying itself. During these instants the living imagination covers the entire field of experience and overruns the contours of the individual life or death. It touches the waiting imagination of the dead.

11. What is the relation of the dead to what has not yet happened, to the future? All the future *is* the construction in which their 'imagination' is engaged.

12. How do the living live with the dead? Until the dehumanization of society by capitalism, all the living awaited the experience of the dead. It was their ultimate future. By themselves the living were incomplete. Thus living and dead were interdependent. Always. Only a uniquely modern form of egoism has broken this interdependence. With disastrous results for the living, who now think of the dead as the *eliminated.*

Wanting Now

(April 2006)

T HE WORLD HAS changed. Information is being commu-
nicated differently. Misinformation is developing its tech-
niques. On a world scale emigration has become the principal
means of survival. The national state of those who had suffered
the worst genocide in history has become, militarily speaking,
fascist. National states in general have been politically down-
sized and reduced to the role of vassals serving the new world
economic order. The visionary political vocabulary of three
centuries has been garbaged. In short, the economic and military global tyranny of today has been established.

At the same time new methods of resistance to this tyranny
are being discovered. Rebels now have to be not so much
obedient as self-reliant. Within the growing opposition
centralized authority has been replaced by spontaneous co-
operation. Long-term programmes are replaced by urgent
alliances over specific issues. Civil society is learning and beginning to practice the guerrilla tactics of political resistance.

7

Today the desire for justice is multitudinous. This is to say that struggles against injustice, struggles for survival, for self-respect, for human rights, should never be considered merely in terms of their immediate demands, their organizations, or their historical consequences. They cannot be reduced to 'movements'. A movement describes a mass of people collectively moving towards a definite goal, which they either achieve or fail to achieve. Yet such a description ignores, or does not take into account, the countless personal choices, encounters, illuminations, sacrifices, new desires, griefs and, finally, memories, which the movement brought about, but which are, in the strict sense, incidental to that movement.

The promise of a movement is its future victory; whereas the promises of the incidental moments are instantaneous. Such moments include, life-enhancingly or tragically, experiences of freedom in action. (Freedom without actions does not exist.) Such moments – as no historical 'outcome' can ever be – are transcendental, are what Spinoza termed eternal, and they are as multitudinous as the stars in an expanding universe.

Not all desires lead to freedom, but freedom is the experience of a desire being acknowledged, chosen and pursued. Desire never concerns the mere possession of something, but the changing of something. Desire is a wanting. A wanting now. Freedom does not constitute the fulfilment of that wanting, but the acknowledgement of its supremacy.

Today the infinite is beside the poor.

Seven Levels of Despair

(November 2001)

I WOULD LIKE – simply as a storyteller – to add a few short remarks to the current debate.

Being a unique Super-Power undermines the military intelligence of strategy. To think strategically one has to imagine oneself in the enemy's place. Then it is possible to foresee, to make feints, to take by surprise, to outflank, etc. Misinterpreting an enemy can lead, in the long run, to defeat – one's own. This is how sometimes empires fall.

A crucial question today is: what makes a world terrorist and, in extremity, what makes a suicide martyr? (I speak here of the anonymous volunteers: Terrorist Leaders are another story.) What makes a terrorist is, first, a form of despair. Or, to put it more accurately, it is a way of transcending and, by the gift of one's own life, making sense of a form of despair.

This is why the term suicide is somewhat inappropriate, for the transcendence gives to the martyr a sense of triumph. A triumph over those he is supposed to hate? I doubt it. The triumph is over the passivity, the bitterness, the sense of absurdity which emanate from a certain depth of despair.

It is hard for the First World to imagine such despair. Not so much because of its relative wealth (wealth produces its own despairs), but because the First World is being continually distracted and its attention diverted. The despair to which I refer comes to those suffering conditions which oblige them to be single-minded. Decades lived in a refugee camp, for example.

This despair consists of what? The sense that your life and the lives of those close to you count for nothing. And this is felt on several different levels so that it becomes total. That is to say, as in totalitarianism, without appeal.

> To search each morning
> to find the scraps
> with which to survive another day.

> The knowledge on waking
> that in this legal wilderness
> no rights exist.

> The experience over the years
> of nothing getting better
> only worse.
> The humiliation of being able
> to change almost nothing,

and of seizing upon the almost
which then leads to another impasse.

The listening to a thousand promises
which pass inexorably
beside you and yours.

The example of those who resist
being bombarded to dust.

The weight of your own killed
a weight which closes
innocence for ever
because they are so many.

These are seven levels of despair – one for each day of
the week – which lead, for some of the more courageous,
to the revelation that to offer one's own life in contesting
the forces which have pushed the world to where it is, is
the only way of invoking an *all*, which is larger than that
of the despair.

Any strategy planned by political leaders to whom such
despair is unimaginable will fail, and will recruit more and
more enemies.

Undefeated Despair

(December 2005)

H OW IS IT I am still alive? I'll tell you I'm alive because there's a temporary shortage of death. This is said with a grin, which is on the far side of a longing for normalcy, for an ordinary life.

Everywhere one goes in Palestine – even in rural areas – one finds oneself amongst rubble, picking a way through, round and over it. At a checkpoint, around some greenhouses which lorries can no longer reach, along any street, going to any rendezvous.

The rubble is of houses, roads and the debris of daily lives. There's scarcely a Palestinian family that has not been forced during the last half century to flee from somewhere, just as there's scarcely a town in which buildings are not regularly bulldozed by the occupying army.

There's also the rubble of words – the rubble of words that house nothing any more, whose sense has been destroyed. Notoriously, the IDF – the Israeli Defence Force, as the Israeli army is called – has become, de facto, an army of conquest. As Sergio Yahni, one of the inspiringly courageous Israeli Refusniks (they refuse to serve in the Army) writes: 'This army does not exist to bring security to the citizens of Israel: it exists to guarantee the continuation of the theft of Palestinian land'.

There is the rubble too of sober and principled words which are being ignored. UN resolutions and the International Court of Justice in the Hague have condemned the building of Israeli settlements on Palestinian territory (there are now nearly half a million such 'settlers') and the construction of the 'separation fence', which is an 8-metre high concrete wall, as illegal. The Occupation and Wall nevertheless continue. Every month the IDF's stranglehold across the territories is tightened. The stranglehold is geographic, economic, civic and military.

All this is clear; it is not happening in some remote, war-locked corner of the globe; every Foreign Office of every rich nation is watching and not one takes measures to discourage the illegalities. 'For us,' a Palestinian mother says at a checkpoint after an IDF soldier has lobbed a tear gas bomb behind her, 'for us the silence of the West is worse' – she nods towards the armoured car – 'than their bullets.'

A gap between declared principles and realpolitik may be a constant throughout history. Often the declarations are grandiloquent. Here, however, it's the opposite. The words are far smaller than the events. What is happening is the careful destruction of a people and a promised nation. And around this destruction there are small words and evasive silence.

For the Palestinians one word remains undiminished: *Nakbah*, meaning 'Catastrophe' and referring to the forced exodus of 700,000 Palestinians in 1948. 'Ours is a country of words. Talk. Talk. Let me rest my road against a stone,' wrote the poet Mahmoud Darwish. *Nakbah* has become a name that four generations share, and it endures so persistently because the operation of 'ethnic cleansing' it names is still largely unacknowledged by Israel and the West. The brave work of the upstanding (and persecuted) new Israeli historians – like Ilan Pappé – is of the utmost importance in this context, for it may lead eventually to such an official acknowledgement, and this would change the fatal name back into a word, however tragic that word.

A familiarity here with every sort of rubble, including the rubble of words.

One tends to forget the geographical scale of the tragedy in question; its scale has become part of the tragedy. The whole of the West Bank plus the Gaza Strip is smaller than Crete (the island from which Palestinians may originally have come in prehistory). Three and a half million people, six times as many as in Crete, live here. And systematically each day the area is being rendered smaller. The towns becoming more and more overcrowded, the countryside more fenced in and inaccessible.

The Settlements extend or new ones begin. Special high-ways for settlers, forbidden to Palestinians, transform old roads into dead-ends. The checkpoints and tortuous ID controls have seriously reduced for most Palestinians the possibility of travelling or even planning to travel within what remains of their own territories. Many can go no further than twenty kilometres in any direction.

The Wall enclaves, cuts off corners (when finished it will have filched nearly 10 per cent of what remains of Palestinian land), fragments the countryside and separates Palestinians from Palestinians. Its aim is to break up Crete into a dozen little islands. The aim of a sledgehammer carried out by bulldozers.

'There is nothing left of us in the wilderness save what the wilderness kept for itself.' (Mahmoud Darwish)

Despair without fear, without resignation, without a sense of defeat, makes for a stance towards the world, here, such as I have never seen before. It may be expressed in one way by a young man joining the Islamic Jihad, in another by an old woman remembering and murmuring through the gaps between her few teeth, and in yet another by a smiling eleven-year-old girl who wraps up a promise to hide it in the despair . . .

This stance, as you call it, how does it work?

Listen . . .

Three boys squatting and playing marbles in the corner of an alley in a refugee camp. In this camp many of the refugees originally came from Haifa. The dexterity with which the boys flick a marble with one thumb, the rest of the body motionless, is not unconnected with the familiarity of very cramped spaces.

Three metres down the alleyway, which is narrower than any hotel corridor, is a shop selling second-hand bicycle parts. All the handlebars are arranged on one hanger, all the back wheels on another, the saddles on a third. If it wasn't for their arrangement, the pieces would look like unsellable scrap. As it is, they sell.

On the wall of a low building with a metal door, opposite the shop, is written: 'From the womb of the camp a revolution is born every day.' A schoolteacher lives with his sister in the two rooms behind the metal door. He indicates the floor of another room which was the size of two bath-tubs. The ceiling and walls have fallen down. That's the room where I was born, he says.

Return to his present living room. He points to a photo in a gilded frame which is hanging on the wall beside an official portrait of Arafat wearing his *keffiyeh*. The framed photo there is my father as a young man, it was taken in Haifa! A colleague told me once he looks like Pasternak, the Russian poet, what do you think? (He does.) He had a heart complaint and the Nakbah killed him. He died in this very room when I was twelve.

At the far end of the building with the metal door, opposite the shop of bicycle parts, eight paces away from where the boys are playing marbles in the corner, there's a square metre of open earth where a jasmine bush is growing. It has only two white flowers, for it's November. Around its root, chucked there from the alley, are a dozen empty plastic mineral water bottles. At least 60 per cent of the camp inhabitants are unemployed. The camps are shantytowns.

When somebody has the opportunity to leave a camp and cross the rubble to slightly better accommodation, it can happen that they turn it down and choose to stay. In the camp they are a member, like a finger, of an endless body. Moving out would be an amputation. The stance of undefeated despair works like this.

Listen . . .

The olive trees on the topmost terrace look tousled; the silver undersides of their leaves are far more visible than usual. This is because yesterday their olives were picked. Last year the crop was poor, the trees tired. This year is better. According to their girth, the trees must be around three or four centuries old. The terraces of dry limestone are probably older.

A couple of kilometres away to the west and south are two recently built settlements. Regular, compact, urban (the settlers commute each day to work in Israel), impenetrable. Neither looks like a village, more like a huge jeep, large enough on the ground to house comfortably two hundred settlers with guns. Both are illegal, both are built on hills, both have lookout towers slender as a mosque's minaret. Their virtual message to the surrounding countryside is: Hands above the head, above the head I told you, and walk slowly backwards.

Building the settlement towards the west and the road leading to it involved the cutting down of several hundred olive trees. The men working on the site were mostly out-of-work Palestinians. The stance of undefeated despair works like this.

The families, who picked their olives yesterday, come from the straggling village in the valley between the two settlements, with a population of about 3,000. Twenty men from the village are in Israeli prisons. One was released two days ago. Several of the young have recently joined Hamas. Many more will vote for Hamas next January. All the kids have toy pistols. All the young grandmothers, whilst wondering what became of the promises they once wrapped, nod in approval at their sons, daughters-in-law, nephews, and worry every night. The stance of undefeated despair works like this.

The Muqata, Arafat's headquarters in the Palestinian capital of Ramallah, was a gigantic heap of rubble three years ago when he was held hostage there by the IDF's tanks and artillery. Now, one year after his death, the Palestinians have cleared the rubble – some argued that it should have been left as an historic monument – and the inner quadrangle is today as bare as a drilling square. On its western side, at ground level, an austere plinth marks Arafat's grave. Above it, a roof like the roof above the platform of a small railway station.

Anybody can find their way there, passing by scarred walls and under garlands of barbed wire. Two sentinels stand guard over the plinth. Apart from them, no head of a (promised) state has a more reticent last resting-place – it simply declares itself to be there against all odds!

If you happen to be standing by his feet when the sun sets, its radiance is that of a silence. He was nicknamed The Walking Catastrophe. Are loved leaders ever pure? Aren't they always full of faults, not weaknesses, flagrant faults? Is this maybe a condition for being a loved leader? Under his leadership the Palestinian Liberation Organization also contributed, on occasion, to the rubble of words. Yet into Arafat's faults were stuffed, like notes into a pocket, the daily wrongs his country suffered. Like this he assumed and carried those wrongs, and their pain found a home, a painful home, in his faults. It's neither purity nor strength that wins such undying loyalty, but something flawed – as each one of us is flawed. The stance of undefeated despair works like this.

The north-west town of Qalqilya (population 50,000) is totally surrounded by seventeen kilometres of the Wall with only one exit. The once bustling main street now ends in the Wall's wasteland. The town's meagre economy is consequently in ruins. A market gardener trundles a wheelbarrow of sand to distribute around some plants before the coming winter. Until the Wall he employed twelve workers (95 per cent of Palestinian businesses have fewer than five employees). Today he employs nobody. The sales of his plants – because the town has been cut off – have been reduced by nine-tenths. He throws away instead

of collecting the seeds from a heap of lychnis flowers. His large hands are heavy with the admission that henceforth here they have nothing to do.

Difficult to convey the sight of the Wall where it crosses the land where there is nobody. It's the opposite of rubble. It is bureaucratic – carefully planned on electronic maps, prefabricated and pre-emptive. Its purpose is to prevent the creation of a Palestinian State. The aim of the sledge-hammer. Since it began to be built three years ago, there has been no significant reduction in the number of kamikaze attacks. Standing before it, you feel as short as a cigarette butt. (Except during Ramadan, most Palestinians smoke a lot.) Yet, oddly, it doesn't look final, only insurmountable.

When it's finished, it will be the 640-kilometre-long expressionless face of an inequality. At the moment it's 210 kilometres long. The inequality is between those who have the full arsenal of the latest military technology to defend what they believe to be their interest (Apache helicopters, Merkava tanks, F16s, etc.) and those who have nothing, save their names and a shared belief that justice is axiomatic. The stance of undefeated despair works like this.

It could be that the Wall belongs to the same short-sighted repressive logic as the 'sonic boom' bombing that the inhabitants of Gaza are being subjected to every night as I write. Jet fighters fly very low at full speed to break the sound barrier, and the nerves of those huddling sleepless below with their axiom. And it won't work.

Such a superiority of firepower discourages intelligent strategy; to think strategically one has to be able to imagine oneself in one's opponent's place, and an habitual sense of superiority precludes this.

Climb one of the jabals and look down at the Wall, way below winding its geometric divider's course towards the southern horizon. Did you see the hoopoe bird? In the long-term view the Wall looks makeshift.

There are 8,000 political prisoners in Israeli jails, 350 of them under eighteen years old. A period in prison has become a normal phase to be undergone, once or several times, in a man's life. Throwing stones can lead to a sentence of two and a half years or more.

Prison for us is a sort of education, a strange sort of university. The man speaking has glasses, is about fifty and is wearing a business-lunch suit. You learn how to learn there. He's the youngest of five brothers and imports coffee-machines. You learn how to struggle together and become inseparable. Certain conditions have improved over the last forty years – improved thanks to us and our hunger strikes. The most I did was twenty days. We won a quarter of an hour more exercise time each day. In the long-sentence prisons they used to mask the windows so there was no sunshine in the cells. We won back some sunshine. We got one body-search removed from the daily routine. Otherwise, we read and discuss what we read, teach each other different languages. And come to know certain soldiers and some of

the guards. In the streets it's the language of bullets and stones between us. Inside it's different. They're in prison just as we are. The difference is we believe in what's got us there, and they mostly don't, because they're just there to earn a living. I know of some friendships that began like that.

The stance of undefeated despair works like this.

The Judean desert between Jerusalem and Jericho is of sandstone, not sand, and is precipitous, not flat. In the spring, parts of it are covered with wild grasses and the goats of Bedouins can feed off it. Later in the year there are only clumps of boxthorn.

If you contemplate this desert, you quickly discover that it's a landscape whose gaze is totally directed towards the sky. A question of geology, not biblical history. It hangs there beneath the sky like a hammock. And when it's windy it twists like a winding sheet. As a result, the sky appears to be more substantial, more urgent, than the land. A porcupine quill blown by the wind lands at your feet. It's not surprising that hundreds of prophets, including the greatest, nurtured their visions here.

The light is fading and a herd of two hundred goats, with a Bedouin shepherd on a mule with his dog, is making its evening zigzag descent down to the camp, where there's water to drink and some extra grain to eat. The thistles and rhizome roots give little nourishment at this time of year.

The difficulty with prophets and their final prophesies is that they tend to ignore what immediately follows an action, ignore consequences. Actions for them, instead of being instrumental, become symbolic. It can happen that prophesies cause people not to see what time contains.

The Bedouin family below are living in two abandoned buildings, not far from a Roman aqueduct. At this time of day the mother will be cooking flat bread, daily bread, on a heated stone. Seven of her sons, who were born here, work with the herd. The family has recently been informed by the IDF that they have to leave before next spring. Hands above the head and walk backwards! All the female goats are pregnant. Five months' gestation period. We'll face that when we get there, says one of the sons. The stance of undefeated despair works like this.

A refusal to see immediate consequences. For example – the Wall and the annexation of still more Palestinian land cannot promise security for the state of Israel; it recruits martyrs.

For example – if a kamikaze martyr could see with their own eyes, before he or she died, the immediate consequences of their explosion, they might well reconsider the appropriateness of their steadfast decision.

The goddamned future of prophesies that ignore all but the final moment!

In the stance I keep referring to, there is something special, a quality which no post-modern or political vocabulary today can find a word for. The quality of a way of sharing which disarms the leading question of: why was one born into this life?

This way of sharing disarms and answers the question not with a promise, or a consolation, or an oath of vengeance – these forms of rhetoric are for the small or large leaders who make History – and this way disarmingly answers the question despite history. Its answer is brief, brief but perpetual. One was born into this life to share the time that repeatedly exists between moments: the time of Becoming, before Being risks to confront one yet again with undefeated despair.

I Would Softly Tell My Love

(January 2002)

Friday.

Nazim, I'm in mourning and I want to share it with you, as you shared so many hopes and so many mournings with us.

> The telegram came at night,
> > only three syllables:
> 'He is dead.'[1]

I'm mourning my friend Juan Muñoz, a wonderful artist, who makes sculptures and installations and who died yesterday on a beach in Spain, aged forty-eight.

I want to ask you about something which puzzles me. After a natural death, as distinct from victimization, killing or dying from hunger, there is first the shock, unless the person has been ailing for a long while, then there is the monstrous sense of loss, particularly when the person is young —

The day is breaking
but my room
is composed of a long night.[2]

– and there follows the pain, which says of itself that it will
never end. Yet with this pain there comes, surreptitiously,
something else which approaches a joke but is not one.
(Juan was a good joker.) Something which hallucinates, a
little similar to the gesture of a conjuror's handkerchief after
a trick, a kind of lightness, totally opposed to what one is
feeling. You recognize what I mean? Is this lightness a frivolity
or a new instruction?

Five minutes after my asking you this, I received a fax from
my son Yves, with some lines he had just written for Juan:

You always appeared
        with a laugh
and a new trick.

You always disappeared
        leaving your hands
on our table.
You disappeared
        leaving your cards
in our hands.

You will re-appear
        with a new laugh
which will be a trick.

Saturday.

I'm not sure whether I ever saw Nazim Hikmet. I would swear to it that I did, but I can't find the circumstantial evidence. I believe it was in London in 1954. Four years after he had been released from prison, nine years before his death. He was speaking at a political meeting held in Red Lion Square. He said a few words and then he read some poems. Some in English, others in Turkish. His voice was strong, calm, highly personal and very musical. But it did not seem to come from his throat — or not from his throat at that moment. It was as though he had a radio in his breast, which he switched on and off with one of his large, slightly trembling hands. I'm describing it badly because his presence and sincerity were very obvious. In one of his long poems he describes six people in Turkey listening in the early 1940s to a symphony by Shostakovich on the radio. Three of the six people are (like him) in prison. The broadcast is live; the symphony is being played at that same moment in Moscow, several thousand kilometres away. Hearing him read his poems in Red Lion Square, I had the impression that the words he was saying were also coming from the other side of the world. Not because they were difficult to understand (they were not), nor because they were blurred or weary (they were full of the capacity of endurance), but because they were being said to somehow triumph over distances and to transcend endless separations. The *here* of all his poems is elsewhere.

In Prague a cart —
                        a one-horse wagon
                passes the Old Jewish Cemetery.
The cart is full of longing for another city,
                        I am the driver.[3]

Even when he was sitting on the platform before he got up to speak, you could see he was an unusually large and tall man. It was not for nothing that he was nicknamed 'The tree with blue eyes'. When he did stand up, you had the impression he was also very light, so light that he risked to become airborne.

Perhaps I never did see him, for it would seem unlikely that, at a meeting organized in London by the international Peace movement, Hikmet would have been tethered to the platform by several guy-ropes so that he should remain earthbound. Yet that is my clear memory. His words after he pronounced them rose into the sky – it was a meeting outdoors – and his body made as if to follow the words he had written, as they drifted higher and higher above the Square and above the sparks of the one-time trams which had been suppressed three or four years before along Theobald's Road.

You're a mountain village
                        in Anatolia,
you're my city,
                        most beautiful and most unhappy.
You're a cry for help – I mean, you're my country;
        the footsteps running towards you are mine.[4]

Monday morning.

Nearly all the contemporary poets who have counted most for me during my long life I have read in translation, seldom in their original language. I think it would have been impossible for anyone to say this before the twentieth century. Arguments about poetry being or not being translatable went on for centuries – but they were chamber arguments – like chamber music. During the twentieth century most of the chambers were reduced to rubble. New means of communication, global politics, imperialisms, world markets, etc., threw millions of people together and took millions of people apart in an indiscriminate and quite unprecedented way. And as a result the expectations of poetry changed; more and more the best poetry counted on readers who were further and further away.

> Our poems
> like milestones
> must line the road.[5]

During the twentieth century, many naked lines of poetry were strung between different continents, between forsaken villages and distant capitals. You all know it, all of you; Hikmet, Brecht, Vallejo, Atilla Jósef, Adonis, Juan Gelman . . .

Monday afternoon.

When I first read some poems by Nazim Hikmet I was in my late teens. They were published in an obscure international literary review in London, which was published under the aegis of the British Communist Party. I was a regular reader. The Party line on poetry was crap, but the poems and stories published were often inspiring.

By that time, Meyerhold had already been executed in Moscow. If I think particularly now of Meyerhold, it is because Hikmet admired him, and was much influenced by him when he first visited Moscow in the early 1920s . . .

'I owe very much to the theatre of Meyerhold. In 1925 I was back in Turkey and I organized the first Workers' Theatre in one of the industrial districts of Istanbul. Working in this theatre as director and writer, I felt that it was Meyerhold who had opened to us new possibilities of working for and with the audience.'

After 1937, those new possibilities had cost Meyerhold his life, but in London readers of the Review did not yet know this.

What struck me about Hikmet's poems when I first discovered them was their space; they contained more space than any poetry I had until then read. They didn't describe space; they came through it, they crossed mountains. They were also about action. They related doubts, solitude, bereavement, sadness, but these feelings followed actions rather than being a substitute for action. Space and actions go together. Their antithesis is prison, and it was in Turkish prisons that Hikmet, as a political prisoner, wrote half his life's work.

Wednesday.

Nazim, I want to describe to you the table on which I'm writing. A white metal garden table, such as one might come across today in the grounds of a *yali* on the Bosphorus. This one is on the covered verandah of a small house in a southeast Paris suburb. This house was built in 1938, one of many houses built here at that time for artisans, tradesmen, skilled workers. In 1938 you were in prison. A watch was hanging on a nail above your bed. In the ward above yours three bandits in chains were awaiting their death sentence.

There are always too many papers on this table. Each morning the first thing I do, whilst sipping coffee, is to try to put them back into order. To the right of me there is a plant in a pot, which I know you would like. It has very dark leaves. Their undersurface is the colour of damsons; on top the light has *stained* them dark brown. The leaves are grouped in threes, as if they were night butterflies – and they are the same size as butterflies – feeding from the same flower. The plant's own flowers are very small, pink and as innocent as the voices of kids learning a song in a primary school. It's a kind of giant clover. This particular one came from Poland, where the plant's name is Koniczyna. It was given to me by the mother of a friend who grew it in her garden near the Ukrainian border. She has striking blue eyes and can't stop touching her plants as she walks through the garden or moves around her house, just as some grandmothers can't stop touching their young grand-children's heads.

My love, my rose,
my journey across the Polish plain has begun:
I'm a small boy happy and amazed
a small boy
looking at his first picture book
     of people
        animals
           objects, plants.[6]

In storytelling everything depends upon what follows what. And the truest order is seldom obvious. Trial and error. Often many times. This is why a pair of scissors and a reel of scotch tape are also on the table. The tape is not fitted into one of those gadgets which makes it easy to tear off a length. I have to cut the tape with the scissors. What is hard is finding where the tape ends on the roll, and then unrolling it. I search impatiently, irritably with my finger-nails. Consequently, when once I do find the end, I stick it on to the edge of the table, and I let the tape unroll until it touches the floor, then I leave it hanging there.

At times I walk out of the verandah into the adjoining room where I chat or eat or read a newspaper. A few days ago, I was sitting in this room and something caught my eye because it was moving. A minute cascade of twinkling water was falling, rippling, towards the verandah floor near the legs of my empty chair in front of the table. Streams in the Alps begin with no more than a trickle like this.

A reel of scotch tape stirred by a draught from a window is sometimes enough to move mountains.

Thursday evening.

Ten years ago I was standing in front of a building in Istanbul near the Haydar-Pasha Station, where suspects were interrogated by the police. Political prisoners were held and cross-examined, sometimes for weeks, on the top floor. Hikmet was cross-examined there in 1938.

The building was not planned as a jail but as a massive administrative fortress. It appears indestructible and is built of bricks and silence. Prisons, constructed as such, have a sinister, but often, also, a nervous, makeshift air about them. For example, the prison in Bursa where Hikmet spent ten years was nicknamed 'the stone aeroplane', because of its irregular layout. The staid fortress I was looking at by the station in Istanbul had by contrast the confidence and tranquility of a monument to silence.

Whoever is inside here and whatever happens inside here – the building announced in measured tones – will be forgotten, removed from the record, buried in a crevice between Europe and Asia.

It was then that I understood something about his poetry's unique and inevitable strategy: it had to continually over-reach its own confinement! Prisoners everywhere have always dreamt of the Great Escape, but Hikmet's poetry did not. His poetry, before it began, placed the prison as a small dot on the map of the world.

The most beautiful sea
        hasn't been crossed yet.
The most beautiful child
        hasn't grown up yet.
Our most beautiful days
        we haven't seen yet.
And the most beautiful words I wanted to tell you
        I haven't said yet.

They've taken us prisoner,
they've locked us up:
        me inside the walls,
           you outside.
But that's nothing.
The worst
is when people – knowingly or not –
carry prison inside themselves . . .
Most people have been forced to do this,

honest, hard-working, good people
who deserve to be loved as much as I love you.[7]

His poetry, like a geometry compass, traced circles, sometimes intimate, sometimes wide and global, with only its
sharp point inserted in the prison cell.

Friday morning.

Once I was waiting for Juan Muñoz in an hotel in
Madrid, and he was late because, as I explained, when

he was working hard at night he was like a mechanic under a car, and he forgot about time. When he eventually turned up, I teased him about lying on his back under cars. And later he sent me a joke fax which I want to quote to you, Nazim. I'm not sure why. Maybe the why isn't my business. I'm simply acting as a postman between two dead men.

'I would like to introduce myself to you – I am a Spanish mechanic (cars only, not motorcycles) who spends most of his time lying on his back underneath an engine looking for it! But – and this is the important issue – I make the occasional art work. Not that I am an artist. No. But I would like to stop this nonsense of crawling in and under greasy cars, and become the Keith Richard of the art world. And if this is not possible to work like the priests, half an hour only, and with wine.

'I'm writing to you because two friends (one in Porto and one in Rotterdam) want to invite you and me to the basement of the Boyman's Car Museum and to other cellars (hopefully more alcoholic) in the old town of Porto.

'They also mentioned something about landscape which I did not understand. Landscape! I think maybe it was something about driving and looking around, or looking around whilst driving around . . .

'Sorry Sir, another client just came in. Whoa! A Triumph Spitfire!'

I hear Juan's laughter, echoing in the studio where he is alone with his silent figures.

Friday evening.

Sometimes it seems to me that many of the greatest poems of the twentieth century – written by women as well as men – may be the most fraternal ever written. If so, this has nothing to do with political slogans. It applies to Rilke, who was apolitical; to Borges, who was a reactionary; and to Hikmet, who was a life-long communist. Our century was one of unprecedented massacres, yet the future it imagined (and sometimes fought for) proposed fraternity. Very few earlier centuries made such a proposal.

> These men, Dino,
> who hold tattered shreds of light
> where are they going
> in this gloom, Dino?
> You, me too:
> we are with them, Dino.
> We too Dino
> have glimpsed the blue sky.[8]

Saturday.

Maybe, Nazim, I'm not seeing you this time either. Yet I would swear to it that I am. You are sitting across the table from me on the verandah. Have you ever noticed how the shape of a head often suggests the mode of thinking which habitually goes on inside it?

There are heads which relentlessly indicate speed of calculation. Others which reveal the determined pursuit of old ideas. Many these days betray the incomprehension of continuous loss. Your head – its size and your screwed-up blue eyes – suggests to me the coexistence of many worlds with different skies, one within another, inside it; not intimidating, calm, but used to overcrowding.

I want to ask you about the period we're living today. Much of what you believed was happening in history, or believed should happen, has turned out to be illusory. Socialism, as you imagined it, is being built nowhere. Corporate capitalism advances unimpeded – although increasingly contested – and the twin World Trade Towers have been blown up. The overcrowded world grows poorer every year. Where is the blue sky today that you saw with Dino?

Yes, those hopes, you reply, are in tatters, yet what does this really change? Justice is still a one-word prayer, as Ziggy Marley sings in your time now. The whole of history is about hopes being sustained, lost, renewed. And with new hopes come new theories. But for the overcrowded, for those who have little or nothing except, sometimes, courage and love, hope works differently. Hope is then something to bite on, to put between the teeth. Don't forget this. Be a realist. With hope between the teeth comes the strength to carry on even when fatigue never lets up, comes the strength, when necessary, to choose not to shout at the wrong moment, comes the strength above all not to howl. A person, with hope between her or his teeth, is a brother or sister who commands respect. Those without hope in the real world are condemned to be alone. The best they can offer is only pity. And whether these hopes between the teeth are fresh or tattered makes little difference when it comes to surviving the nights and imagining a new day. Do you have any coffee?

I'll make some.

I leave the verandah. When I come back from the kitchen with two cups – and the coffee is Turkish – you have left. On the table, very near where the scotch tape is stuck, there is a book, open at a poem you wrote in 1962.

If I was a plane tree I would rest in its shade
If I was a book
I'd read without being bored on sleepless nights
Pencil I would not want to be even between my own
 fingers
If I was door
I would open for the good and shut for the wicked
If I was window a wide open window without curtains
I would bring the city into my room
If I was a word
I'd call out for the beautiful the just the true
If I was word
I would softly tell my love.[9]

Where Are We?

(October 2002)

I WANT TO SAY at least something about the pain existing in the world today.

Consumerist ideology, which has become the most powerful and invasive on the planet, sets out to persuade us that pain is an accident, something that we can insure against. This is the logical basis for the ideology's pitilessness.

Everyone knows, of course, that pain is endemic to life, and wants to forget this or relativize it. All the variants of the myth of a Fall from the Golden Age, before pain existed, are an attempt to relativize the pain suffered on earth. So too is the invention of Hell, the adjacent kingdom of pain-as-punishment. Likewise the discovery of Sacrifice. And later, much later, the principle of Forgiveness. One could argue that philosophy began with the question: why pain?

Yet, when all this has been said, the present pain of living in the world is perhaps in some ways unprecedented.

I write in the night, although it is daytime. A day in early

October 2002. For almost a week the sky above Paris has been blue. Each day the sunset is a little earlier and each day gloriously beautiful. Many fear that before long, US military forces will be launching the 'preventive' war against Iraq so that the US oil corporations can lay their hands on further and supposedly safer oil supplies. Others hope that this can be avoided. Between the announced decisions and the secret calculations, everything is kept unclear, since lies prepare the way for missiles. I write in a night of shame.

By shame I do not mean individual guilt. Shame, as I'm coming to understand it, is a species feeling which, in the long run, corrodes the capacity for hope and prevents us looking far ahead. We look down at our feet, thinking only of the next small step.

People everywhere – under very different conditions – are asking themselves – where are we? The question is historical not geographical. What are we living through? Where are we being taken? What have we lost? How to continue without a plausible vision of the future? Why have we lost any view of what is beyond a lifetime?

The well-heeled experts answer: Globalization. Post-Modernism. Communications Revolution. Economic Liberalism. The terms are tautological and evasive. To the anguished question of Where are we? the experts murmur: Nowhere!

Might it not be better to see and declare that we are living through the most tyrannical – because the most pervasive – chaos that has ever existed? It's not easy to grasp the nature of the tyranny, for its power structure (ranging from the 200 largest multinational corporations to the Pentagon) is interlocking yet diffuse, dictatorial yet anonymous, ubiquitous yet placeless. It tyrannizes from off-shore – not only in terms of fiscal law, but in terms of any political control beyond its own. Its aim is to delocalize the entire world. Its ideological strategy – besides which Bin Laden's is a fairy tale – is to undermine the existent so that everything collapses into its special version of the virtual, from the realm of which – and this is the tyranny's credo – there will be a never-ending source of profit. It sounds stupid. Tyrannies are stupid. This one is destroying at every level the life of the planet on which it operates.

Ideology apart, its power is based on two threats. The first is intervention from the sky by the most heavily armed state in the world. One could call it Threat B52. The second is of ruthless indebtment, bankruptcy, and hence, given the present productive relations in the world, starvation. One could call it Threat Zero.

The shame begins with the contestation (which we all acknowledge somewhere but, out of powerlessness, dismiss) that much of the present suffering could be alleviated or avoided if certain realistic and relatively simple decisions were taken. There is a very direct relation today between the minutes of meetings and minutes of agony.

Does anyone deserve to be condemned to certain death simply because they don't have access to treatment which

43

would cost less than two dollars a day? This was a question posed by the Director of the World Health Organization last July. She was talking about the AIDS epidemic in Africa and elsewhere from which an estimated 68 million people will die within the next eighteen years. I'm talking about the pain of living in the present world.

Most analyses and prognoses about what is happening are understandably presented and studied within the framework of their separate disciplines: economics, politics, media studies, public health, ecology, national defence, criminology, education, etc. In reality each of these separate fields is joined to another to make up the real terrain of what is being lived. It happens that in their lives, people suffer from wrongs which are classified in separate categories, whereas they suffer them simultaneously and *inseparably*.

A current example: some Kurds, who fled last week to Cherbourg and have been refused asylum by the French government and risk being repatriated to Turkey, are poor, politically undesirable, landless, exhausted, illegal and the clients of nobody. And they suffer each of these conditions at one and the same second!

To take in what is happening, an interdisciplinary vision is necessary in order to connect the 'fields' which are institutionally kept separate. And any such vision is bound to be (in the original sense of the word) political. The precondition for thinking politically on a global scale is to see the *unity* of the unnecessary suffering taking place.

*

I write in the night, but I see not only the tyranny. If that were so, I would probably not have the courage to continue writing. I see people sleeping, stirring, getting up to drink water, whispering their projects or their fears, making love, praying, cooking something whilst the rest of the family is asleep, in Baghdad and Chicago. (Yes, I see too the forever invincible Kurds, 4,000 of whom were gassed — with US compliance — by Saddam Hussein.) I see pastry cooks working in Teheran and the shepherds, thought of as bandits, sleeping beside their sheep in Sardinia, I see a man in the Friedrichshain quarter of Berlin sitting in his pyjamas with a bottle of beer reading Heidegger and he has the hands of a proletarian, I see a small boat of illegal immigrants off the Spanish coast near Alicante, I see a mother in Mali, her name is Aya which means Born on Friday, swaying her baby to sleep, I see the ruins of Kabul and a man going home, and I know that, despite the pain, the ingenuity of the survivors is undiminished, an ingenuity which scavenges and collects energy, and in the ceaseless cunning of this ingenuity, there is a spiritual value, something like the Holy Ghost. I am convinced of this in the night, although I don't know why.

*

It is a little more than a century ago that Dvořák composed his *Symphony from the New World*. He wrote it whilst directing a Conservatory of Music in New York, and the writing of it inspired him to compose, eighteen months later, still in New York, his sublime *Cello Concerto*. In the *Symphony* the horizons and rolling hills of his native Bohemia become the promises of the New World. Not grandiloquent but loud and continuing, for they correspond to the longings of those without power, of those who are wrongly called simple, of those the USA Constitution addressed in 1787.

I know of no other work of art which expresses so directly and yet so toughly (Dvorák was the son of a peasant and his father dreamed of his becoming a butcher) the beliefs which inspired generation after generation of migrants who became US citizens.

For Dvorák the force of these beliefs were inseparable from a kind of tenderness, a respect for life such as can often be found intimately amongst the governed (as distinct from governors). And it was in this spirit that the *Symphony* was publicly received when it was first performed at Carnegie Hall (16 December 1893).

Dvorák was asked what he thought about the future of American music and he recommended that US composers listen to the music of the Indians and Blacks. The *Symphony from the New World* expressed a hopefulness without frontiers which, paradoxically, is welcoming because centred on an idea of home. An utopian paradox.

Today the power of the same country which inspired such hopes has fallen into the hands of a coterie of fanatical (wanting to limit everything except the power of capital), ignorant (recognizing only the reality of their own fire-power), hypocritical (two measures for all ethical judgments, one for us and another for them) and ruthless B52 plotters.

How did this happen? How did Bush, Murdoch, Cheney,

Kristol, Rumsfeld, et al. get where they did? The question is rhetorical for there is no single answer, and it is idle, for no answer will dent their power yet. But to ask it in this way in the night reveals the enormity of what has happened. We are writing about the pain in the world.

We have to reject the new tyranny's discourse. Its terms are crap. In the interminably repetitive speeches, announcements, press conferences and threats, the recurrent terms are: Democracy, Justice, Human Rights, Terrorism. Each word in the context signifies the opposite of what it was once meant to signify.

Democracy is a proposal (rarely realized) about decision making; it has little to do with election campaigns. Its promise is that political decisions be made after, and in the light of, consultation with the governed. This is dependent upon the governed being adequately informed about the issues in question, and upon the decision-makers having the capacity and will to listen and take account of what they have heard. Democracy should not be confused with the 'freedom' of binary choices, the publication of opinion polls or the crowding of people into statistics. These are its pretences.

Today the fundamental decisions, which effect the unnecessary pain increasingly suffered across the planet, have been and are taken unilaterally without any open consultation or participation.

Both military and economic strategists now realize that the media play a crucial role – not so much in defeating the current enemy as in foreclosing and preventing mutiny, protests or desertion. Any tyranny's manipulation of the media is an index of its fears. The present one lives in fear of the world's desperation. A fear so deep that the adjective desperate – except when it means dangerous – is never used.

Without money each daily human need becomes a pain.

*

Every form of contestation against this tyranny is comprehensible. Dialogue with it is impossible. For us to live and die properly, things have to be named properly. Let us reclaim our words.

This is written in the night. In war the dark is on nobody's side; in love the dark confirms that we are together.

War Against Terrorism
or a Terrorist War?

(June 2002)

WHEN ON 11 SEPTEMBER 2001 I watched the videos on television, I was instantly reminded of 6 August 1945. We in Europe heard the news of the bombing of Hiroshima on the evening of the same day.

The immediate correspondences between the two events include a fireball descending without warning from a clear sky, both attacks being timed to coincide with the civilians of the targeted city going to work in the morning, with the shops opening, with children in school preparing their lessons. A similar reduction to ashes, with bodies flung through the air, becoming debris. A comparable incredulity and chaos provoked by a new weapon of destruction being used for the first time – the A-bomb sixty years ago, and a civil airliner last autumn. Everywhere at the epicentre, on every thing and every body, a thick pall of dust.

The differences of context and scale are of course enormous. In Manhattan the dust was not radioactive. In 1945 the United States had been waging a full-scale war with Japan for three years. Both attacks, however, were planned as announcements.

Watching either, one knew that the world would never again be the same; the risks everywhere, to which life was heir, had been changed on the morning of a new unclouded day.

The bombs dropped on Hiroshima and Nagasaki announced that the United States was henceforth the supreme armed power in the world. The attack of 11 September announced that this power was no longer guaranteed invulnerability on its home ground. The two events mark the beginning and end of a certain historical period.

Concerning President Bush's riposte to 9/11, his so-called 'War on Terror', which was first baptized 'Infinite Justice', and then renamed 'Enduring Freedom', concerning this riposte the most trenchant and anguished comments and analyses I have come across have been made and written by United States citizens. The accusation of 'anti-Americanism' against those of us who adamantly oppose the present decision-makers in Washington is as short-sighted as the policies in question. There are countless anti-American US citizens, with whom we are in solidarity.

There are also many US citizens who support these policies, including the 60 intellectuals who signed a statement which set out to define what is a 'just' war in general, and why in particular the operation Enduring Freedom in

Afghanistan, and the ongoing war against terrorism, are justified.

They argued that the moral justification for a just war is when its purpose is to defend the innocent against evil. They quoted St. Augustine. They added that such a war must respect as far as possible the immunity of non-combatants.

If their text is read innocently (and of course it was not written either spontaneously or innocently), it suggests a patient gathering of erudite, quietly spoken experts, with access to a great library (and perhaps, between sessions, a swimming pool), who have the time and quiet to reflect, to discuss their hesitations, and finally to come to an agreement and offer their judgment. And it suggests that this meeting took place somewhere in a mythic six-star hotel (accessible only by helicopter) in its own spacious grounds, surrounded by high walls with guards and check-points. No contact whatsoever between thinkers and the local populations. No chance meetings. As a result, what really happened in history and what is happening today beyond the walls of the hotel is unadmitted and unknown. Isolated De Luxe Tourist Ethics.

Return to the summer of 1945. Sixty-six of Japan's largest cities had been burnt to the ground by napalm bombing. In Tokyo a million civilians were homeless and 100,000 people had died. They had been, according to Major General Curtis Lemay, who was in charge of the fire-bombing operations, 'scorched and boiled and baked to death'. President

Franklin Roosevelt's son and confidant said that the bombing should continue 'until we have destroyed about half the Japanese civilian population'. On 18 July the Japanese Emperor telegraphed President Truman, who had succeeded Roosevelt, and once again asked for peace. The message was ignored.

A few days before the bombing of Hiroshima, Vice Admiral Radford boasted that 'Japan will eventually be a nation without cities – a nomadic people'.

The bomb, exploding above a hospital in the centre of the city, killed 100,000 people instantly, 95 per cent of them civilians. Another 100,000 died slowly from burns and the effects of radiation.

'Sixteen hours ago,' President Truman announced, 'an American airplane dropped one bomb on Hiroshima, an important Japanese army base.'

One month later the first uncensored report – by the intrepid Australian journalist Wilfred Burchett – described the cataclysmic suffering he encountered after visiting a makeshift hospital in the city.

General Groves, who was the military director of the Manhattan Project for planning and manufacturing the bomb, hastily reassured Congressmen that radiation caused no 'undue suffering' and that 'in fact, they say it is a very pleasant way to die'.

In 1946 the US Strategic Bombing Survey came to the conclusion that 'Japan would have surrendered even if atomic bombs had not been dropped . . .'

*

To describe a sequence of events as briefly as I have is, of course, to over-simplify. The Manhattan Project was started in 1942 when Hitler was triumphant and there was the risk that researchers in Germany might manufacture atomic weapons first. The US decision, when this risk no longer existed, to drop two atomic bombs on Japan, needs to be considered in the shadow of the atrocities committed by Japanese armed forces across South-East Asia, and the surprise attack on Pearl Harbor in December 1941. There were US commanders and certain scientists working on the Manhattan Project who did their best to delay or argue against Truman's fateful decision.

Yet finally, when all was said and done, the unconditional surrender of Japan on 14 August could not have been, and was certainly not, celebrated as the longed-for victory. There was an anguish at the centre of it, and a blindness which blinded.

Let Us Think About Fear

(April 2003)

If we don't succeed, we run the risk of failure.

George W. Bush

B AGHDAD HAS FALLEN. The city has been taken by the troops who were bringing it freedom. Its hospitals are wailingly overcrowded with burnt and maimed civilians, many of them children, and all of them victims of the computerized missiles, shells and bombs launched by the city's liberators. The statues of Saddam Hussein have been overturned. Meanwhile, in the Pentagon at a press conference, Mr. Rumsfeld is suggesting that the next country to be liberated may be Syria.

Early this morning came an e-mail from a friend who is a painter: 'The world today is hard to look at, let alone think of.' All of us can recognize ourselves in that cri de cœur – yet let's think.

There are certain moments of looking at a familiar mountain which are unrepeatable. A question of a particular light, an exact temperature, the wind, the season. You could live seven lives and never see the mountain quite like that again; its face is as specific as a momentary glance across a table at breakfast. A mountain stays in the same place, and can almost be considered immortal, but to those who are familiar with the mountain, it never repeats itself. It has another timescale.

Each day and night of the ongoing war in Iraq is different with different griefs, different acts of defiance, different stupidities. It remains, however, the same war, the war which almost everyone in the world perceived, before it began, as an aggression of unprecedented cynicism (the ravine between declared principles and real aims), undertaken to seize control of one of the world's richest oil reserves, to test out new weapons, like the microwave bomb, weapons of pitiless destruction, many of which were offered free to the Pentagon by the manufacturers in the hope of winning substantial contracts for wars to come, but principally and above all undertaken to demonstrate to the present fragmented but globalized world what 'Shock and Awe' is!

This can be put less rhetorically. The primary aim of the war, launched in defiance of the UN, was to demonstrate what is likely to happen to any leader, nation, community or people who persist in refusing to comply with US interests. Many propositions and memos about the vital need for such a demonstration were being discussed in corporate and operational planning circles before Bush's election, and before the terrorist attacks of 11 September 2001.

The term 'US interests' can lead to confusion here. It does not refer to the direct interest of US citizens, whether poor or well-off, but to the interests of the most extensive multinational corporations, often dominated by US capital, and now, when necessary, defended by US armed forces.

What Rumsfeld, Cheney, Rice, Wolfowitz, Perle and co. have succeeded in doing since 11 September is to close any debate about the legitimacy or ultimate efficacy of such a threatening deployment of power. They have used the fear set off by the Twin Towers attack to try to enlist the media and public opinion in support of unilaterally decided pre-emptive strikes against any target they name terrorist. As a result, the world market with its spin is being woven into the Stars and Stripes, and the making of profit (for the few who can) is becoming the only inalienable right.

'Terrorism is the war of the poor, and war is the terrorism of the rich,' Peter Ustinov the playwright recently observed with succinct clarity.

Although the assertion that Iraq still had weapons of mass destruction was the so-called justification for the country's invasion, there has perhaps never been a war in which the inequality of firepower between the combatants has been so great. On one hand, satellite surveillance night and day, B52s, Tomahawk missiles, cluster bombs, shells with depleted uranium and computerized weapons which are so sophisticated that they give rise to the theory (and virtual dream) of a no-contact war; on the other hand, sandbags, elderly men brandishing the pistols of their youth and handfuls of *fedayeen*, wearing torn shirts and sneakers, armed with a few Kalashnikovs. The majority of the conventionally armed troops of the Republican Guard were bombed out of existence during the first week. The comparative casualty rates between the Iraqi forces and those of the Coalition may turn out to be, as in the operation whose logo was Desert Storm, something approaching 1000:1.

Baghdad was taken within five days of the Land Army being given the order to attack. The obligatory overthrowing of the dictator's hideous statues followed the same pattern; the liberated citizens only had hammers whilst the US troops assisted with tanks and bulldozers.

The speed of the operation convinced the tame journalists, but not the courageous ones, that the invasion was, as promised, a liberation! Might had been demonstrated to be right! Meanwhile, Baghdad's poor, fatally deprived during the eleven-year embargo, started to pillage empty public buildings. The chaos began.

*

Return to the mountain, which proposes another timescale, and observe from there. The victors, with their historically unprecedented superiority of weapons, the victors who were bound to be victors, appeared frightened. Not only the gas-masked marines, dispatched to a problematic country and undergoing real desert storms, but faraway spokespeople in the comfort of the Pentagon, and, above all, the Coalition's national leaders, appearing on TV or conferring, conspiratorially, in out-of-the-way places.

Many of the errors committed during the early stages of the war – soldiers being killed by friendly fire, civilian families being blown to pieces at point-blank range (an operation called 'killing the vehicle') – were said to be caused by over-nervousness.

Any of us can become terrified at any moment if fear waylays us. The leaders of the New World Order, however, would seem to be married to Fear, and their subordinate Commanders and Sergeants to be indoctrinated from above with something of the same fear.

What are the practices of this marriage? Day and night the partners of Fear are anxiously preoccupied with telling themselves and their subordinates the right half-truths, half-truths which hope to change the world from what it is into something which it is not! It takes about six half-truths to make a lie. As a result, they become unfamiliar with reality, whilst continuing to dream about, and of course to exercise, power. They continually have to absorb shocks whilst accelerating. Decisiveness becomes their invariable device for preventing the asking of questions.

Married as they are to Fear, they cannot come to terms with, or find a place for, death. Fear keeps death out, and so the Dead desert them. They are alone on this planet – as the rest of the world is not. This is why, considering all the power they wield, military and otherwise, they are dangerous. Terrifyingly dangerous. It is also why they cannot survive.

On the twenty-third day of the war the chaos increased exponentially. The regime had toppled. Saddam Hussein could not be found. The aerial bombardments continued their havoc wherever General Tommy Franks saw fit. And on the ground in Baghdad and some other liberated cities, everything was being pillaged, stolen, dismembered, not only from deserted ministries, but from shops, houses, hotels, and even hospitals to which more and more of the maimed and dying were being hopelessly carried. Some doctors in Baghdad took up guns to try to defend their services and equipment. Meanwhile the forces who liberated and traumatized the city stood by, astounded, nervous, doing nothing.

The scenario for the jubilant toppling of the Saddam Hussein statues was foreseen in the Pentagon and studiously prepared for, because it contained a half-truth. The whole truth of what is happening in the cities was not foreseen. Mr. Secretary Rumsfeld referred to the chaos as merely 'an untidiness'.

When one tyranny is overthrown, not by the people concerned but by another tyranny, the result risks to be chaos, because it will seem to the people that the ultimate hope of any social order has been totally destroyed, and then the impulse to seize for personal survival takes over and looting begins. It is as simple and terrible as that. Yet the new tyrants know nothing about how people in extremis behave. Their fear stops them knowing; they are alone on this planet; even the dead have deserted them.

Stones

(June 2003)

E QBAL AHMED WAS, I think, a man who saw life whole. He was cunning, quick, had little time to spare for fools, loved cooking, and was the opposite of an opportunist – of somebody who fragments life. I once wrote an account of his childhood in Bihar at the time of the partition of India and Pakistan. It was a version on paper of what he told me one night in a bar in Amsterdam. He asked me when he read it to change his name. Which I did. The story was about what made him decide, at the age of seventeen, to become a revolutionary. Now he's dead, I return his name to him.

Influenced by the writings of Frantz Fanon – and particularly by *The Wretched of the Earth* – he became deeply involved in several liberation struggles, including that of the Palestinians. I remember him talking to me about Jenin. Towards the end of his life, Eqbal set up a freethinking university in Pakistan named after the great fifteenth-century philosopher Ibn Khaldun, who imagined the discipline of sociology before it existed.

Eqbal learnt early on that life inevitably leads to separations. Everybody recognized this before the category of the tragic was discarded as garbage. Eqbal, though, knew and accepted the tragic. And, consequently, he spent much of his prodigious energy on forging links – of friendship, political solidarity, military loyalty, shared poetry, hospitality – links which had a chance of surviving after the inevitable separations. I still remember the meals he cooked.

I didn't expect to encounter Eqbal in Ramallah. Although, oddly, the first book I picked up and opened there had a photo of him on the third page. No, I wasn't looking for him. Yet he had been beside me when I decided to visit the city, and he left me a message which I saw like an SMS on the tiny screen of my imagination.

Look at the stones! it said.

O.K., I replied, the stones, in my own way.

Certain trees – particularly the mulberries and medlars – still tell the story of how long ago, in another life, before the *Nakbah*, Ramallah was, for the well-off, a town of leisure and ease, a place to retreat to from nearby Jerusalem during the hot summers, a resort. The *Nakbah* refers to the 'catastrophe' of 1948 when ten thousand Palestinians were killed and 700,000 were forced to leave their country.

Long ago, newly married couples planted roses in

Ramallah gardens as an augury for their future life together. The alluvial soil suited the roses.

Today there is not a wall in the town centre of Ramallah, now the capital of the Palestinian Authority, which is not covered with photographs of the dead, taken when alive and now reprinted as small posters. The dead are the martyrs of the Second Intifada which began in September 2000. The martyrs include all those killed by the Israeli army and settlers, and those who decided to sacrifice themselves in suicidal counter-attacks. These faces transform the desultory street walls into something as intimate as a wallet of private papers and pictures. The wallet has a pocket for the magnetic ID card issued by the Israeli security services and without which no Palestinian can travel even a few kilometres, and another pocket for eternity. Around the posters, the walls are scarred with bullet and shrapnel marks.

There is an old woman, who might be the grandmother in several wallets. There are boys in their early teens, there are many fathers. Listening to the stories of how they met their death, one is reminded of what poverty is about. Poverty forces the hardest choices which lead to almost nothing. Poverty is living with that *almost*.

Most of the boys, whose faces are on the walls, were born in refugee camps, as poor as shantytowns. They left school early to earn money for the family or help the father with his job, if he had one. A few dreamt of becoming wizard soccer players. A fair number of them made catapults of carved wood, twined rope and twisted leather for hurling stones at the Occupying Army.

Any comparison between the weapons involved in these confrontations returns us to what poverty is about. On one hand Apache and Cobra helicopters, F16s, Abrams tanks, Humvee jeeps, electronic surveillance systems, tear gas; on the other hand catapults, slingshots, mobile telephones, badly used Kalashnikovs and mostly handmade explosives. The enormity of the contrast reveals something which I can feel between these grief-stricken walls but which I cannot put a name to. If I was an Israeli soldier, however well-armed I was, I might finally be frightened of this something. Perhaps it's what the poet Mourid Barghouti noticed: 'Living people grow old but martyrs grow younger.'

Three stories from the walls.

Husni Al-Nayjar, fourteen years old. He worked helping his father, who was a welder. Whilst flinging stones, he was shot dead with a bullet to the head. In his photo he gazes calmly and unwaveringly into the middle distance.

Abdelhamid Kharti, thirty-four years old. Painter and writer. When young, he had trained as a medical nurse. He volunteered to join a medical emergency unit for rescuing and taking care of the wounded. His corpse was found near a checkpoint, after a night when there had been no confrontations. His fingers had been cut off. A thumb was hanging loose. An arm, a hand and his jaw were broken. There were twenty bullets in his body.

Muhammad Al-Durra, twelve years old, lived in the Breij Camp. He was returning home with his father across the Netzarim checkpoint in Gaza and they were ordered to get out of their vehicle. Soldiers were already shooting. The two of them took immediate cover behind a cement wall. The father waved to show they were there and was shot in the hand. A little later Muhammad was shot in the foot. The father now shielded his son with his own body. More bullets hit both, and the boy was killed. Doctors removed eight bullets from the father's body, but he remained paralyzed as a consequence of the wounds and could no longer work, remaining unemployed. Because the incident happened to be filmed, the story is told and retold across the world.

I want to do a drawing for Abdelhamid Kharti. Very early in the morning we go to the village of Ain Kinya and beyond it there's a Bedouin encampment, near a wadi. The sun is not yet hot. The goats and sheep are grazing more or less between the tents. I've chosen to draw the hills looking eastwards. I sit on a rock near a small blackish tent. I have only a notebook and this pen. There's a discarded plastic mug on the earth and it gives me the idea of fetching some water from the trickle of the spring to mix, when necessary, with my ink.

After I've been drawing for a while, a young man (every invisible person in the camp has of course noticed me) approaches, undoes the entrance to the tent behind me, enters and comes out holding up a decrepit white plastic stool which, he indicates, might be more comfortable than the rock. I guess that before he found it, it must have been thrown out into the street by some pastry shop or ice-cream parlour. I thank him.

And sitting on this customer's stool in the Bedouin camp, as the sun gets hotter and the frogs in the almost dry riverbed begin to croak, I go on drawing.

On a hilltop, a few kilometres to the left, is an Israeli settlement. It looks military, as if it were part of a weapon designed for quick handling. Yet it's small and faraway.

The near limestone hill facing me has the form of a gigantic sleeping animal's head, the rocks scattered on it like burrs in its matted hair. Suddenly frustrated by my lack of pigment, I pour water from the mug on to the dust at my feet, dip my finger into the mud and smear colour across the drawing of the animal's head. The sun is hot now. A mule brays. I turn the pages of the notebook to begin another and another. Nothing looks finished. When the young man eventually returns, he wants to see my drawings.

I hold up the open notebook. He smiles. I turn a page. He points. Ours, he says, our dust! He's pointing at my finger, not the drawing.

Then we both look at the hill.

I am among not the conquered but the defeated, whom the victors fear. The time of the victors is always short and that of the defeated unaccountably long. Their space is different too. Everything in this limited land is a question of space, and the victors have understood this. The stranglehold they maintain is first and foremost spatial. It is applied, illegally and in defiance of international law, through the checkpoints, through the destruction of ancient roads, through the new by-passes strictly reserved for Israeli settlers, through the fortress hilltop settlements, which are really surveillance and control points of the surrounding plateaux, through the curfew which obliges people to stay indoors night and day until it is lifted. During the invasion of Ramallah last year, the curfew lasted six weeks, with a 'lifting' of a couple of hours on certain days for shopping. There was not even enough time to bury those who died in their beds.

The dissenting Israeli architect Eyal Weizman has pointed out in a courageous book that this total terrestrial domination begins in the drawings of district-planners and architects. The violence begins long before the arrival of the tanks and jeeps. He talks of a 'politics of verticality', whereby the defeated even when 'at home' are being literally *overseen* and *undermined*.

The effect of this on daily life is relentless. As soon as somebody one morning says to himself 'I'll go and see –' he has to stop short and check how many crossings of barriers the 'outing' is likely to involve. The space of the simplest everyday decisions is hobbled, with its foreleg tethered to its hind leg.

In addition, because the barriers change unpredictably from day to day, the experience of time is hobbled. Nobody knows how long it will take this morning to get to work, to go and see Mother, to attend a class, to consult the doctor, nor, having done these things, how long it will take to get back home. The trip, in either direction, may take thirty minutes or four hours, or the route may be categorically shut off by soldiers with their loaded submachine guns.

The Israeli government claims that they are obliged to take these measures to combat terrorism. The claim is a feint. The true aim of the stranglehold is to destroy the indigenous population's sense of temporal and spatial continuity so that they either leave or become indentured servants. And it's here that the dead help the living to resist. It's here that men and women make their decision to become martyrs. The stranglehold inspires the terrorism it purports to be fighting.

A small road of stones, negotiating boulders, descending into a valley south of Ramallah. Sometimes it winds between olive groves of old trees, a number of them perhaps dating from Roman times. This rocky track (very hard on any car) is the only means of access for Palestinians to their nearby village. The original asphalt road, forbidden to them now, is reserved for Israelis in the settlements. I walk ahead because all my life I have found it more tiring to walk slowly. I spot a red flower amongst the shrubs and stop to pick it. Later I learn it is called Adonis Aestivalis. Its red is very intense and its life, the botanical book says, brief.

Baha shouts to warn me not to head towards the high hill on my left. If they spot someone approaching, he shouts, they shoot.

I try to calculate the distance: less than a kilometre. A couple of hundred metres away in the unrecommended direction I spot a tethered mule and horse. I take them as a guarantee and I walk there.

Where I arrive, two boys – aged about eleven and eight – are working alone in a field. The younger one is filling watering cans from a barrel buried in the earth. The care with which he does so, not spilling a drop, shows how precious the water is. The elder boy takes the full can and carefully climbs down to a ploughed plot where he is watering plants. Both of them are barefoot.

The one watering beckons to me and proudly shows me the rows of several hundred plants on the plot. Some I recognize: tomatoes, aubergines, cucumbers. They must have been planted during the last week. They're still small, searching for water. One plant I don't recognize and he notices this. Big light, he says. Melon? Shumaam! We laugh. His laughing eyes fixed on me don't waver. (I think of Husni Al-Nayjar.) We are both – God knows why – living at the same moment. He takes me down the rows to show me how much he has watered. At one moment we pause, look around and glance at the settlement with its defensive walls and red roofs. As he points with his chin in its direction there is a kind of derision in his gesture, a derision which he wants to share with me, like his pride in watering. A derision which gives way to a grin – as if we had both agreed to piss at the same moment at the same spot.

Later we walk back towards the rocky road. He picks some short mint and hands me a bunch. Its pungent fresh-ness is like a draught of cold water, water colder than that in the watering can. We are going towards the horse and mule. The horse, unsaddled, has a halter with reins but neither bridle nor bit. He wants to demonstrate to me something more impressive than an imaginary piss. He leaps onto the horse whilst his brother reassures the mule, and almost instantly he is galloping, bareback, down the road from which I came. The horse has six legs, four of its own and two belonging to its rider, and the boy's hands control all six. He rides with the experience of several lifetimes. When he returns, he is grinning and, for the first time, looks shy.

I rejoin Baha and the others, who are a kilometre away. They are talking to a man, who is the boy's uncle, and who is likewise watering plants which have been recently bedded out. The sun is going down and the light is changing. The brownish yellow earth, which is darker where it has been watered, is now the primary colour of the whole landscape. He is using the last of the water in the bottom of a 500-litre dark blue plastic barrel.

On the surface of the blue barrel eleven patches – like those used for mending punctures but larger – have been carefully stuck. The man will explain to me that this is how he repaired the barrel after a gang from the settlement of Halamish, the settlement with red roofs, came one night, when they knew the water containers were full of spring rain, and slashed them with knives. Another barrel, lying on the terrace below, was irreparable. Further off on the same terrace stands the gnarled stump of an olive tree, which, to judge by its girth, must have been several hundred, perhaps a thousand, years old.

A few nights ago, the uncle says, they cut it down with a chain saw.

I quote again from Mourid Barghouti: 'For the Palestinian, olive oil is the gift of the traveller, the comfort of the bride, the reward of autumn, the boast of the storeroom and the wealth of the family across centuries.'

Later, I find a poem by Zakaria Mohammed called The Bit. It talks about a black horse without a bridle which has blood dripping from its lips. With Zakaria's horse too there is a boy, astonished by the blood.

> What is the black horse chewing?
> he asks,
> What does it chew?
> The black horse
> is biting
> a bit forged from steel
> a bit of memory
> to be champed on
> champed on until death.

If the boy who gave me the short mint was seven years older, it wouldn't be hard to imagine why he joined Hamas, ready to sacrifice his life.

The weight of the smashed concrete slabs and fallen masonry of Arafat's wrecked compound in the centre of Ramallah has taken on a symbolic gravity. Not, however, in the way the Israeli commanders imagined. Smashing the Muqata with Arafat and his company in it was for them a public demonstration of his humiliation, just as in the private apartments which the army systematically raided and searched, the tomato ketchup smeared on to clothes, furniture and walls was a private warning of worse to come.

Arafat still represents the Palestinians more faithfully perhaps than any other world leader represents his people. Not democratically but tragically. Hence the gravity. Due to the many errors committed by the PLO, with him at its head, and due to the equivocations of the surrounding Arab states, he has no room left for political manoeuvre. He has ceased to be a political leader. Yet he remains defiantly here. Nobody believes in him. And many would give their lives for him. How is this? No longer a politician, Arafat has become a rubble mountain, but a mountain of the homeland.

I have never seen such a light before. It comes down from the sky in a strangely regular way, for it makes no distinction between what is distant and what is close. The difference between far and near is one of scale, never of colour, texture or precision. And this affects the way you place yourself, it affects your sense of being here. The land arranges itself around you, rather than confronting you. It's the opposite of Arizona. Instead of beckoning, it recommends never leaving.

And so I am here, a figure in a dream that some of my ancestors in Poland, Galicia and the Austro-Hungarian Empire must have nurtured and spoken about for at least two centuries. And here I unhesitatingly identify myself with the just cause and the pain of those whom the state of Israel (and cousins of mine) are afflicting to a degree that is tragically totalitarian.

Riad, who is a teacher of carpentry, has gone to fetch his drawings to show me. We are sitting in the garden of his father's house. The father with his white horse is harrowing the field opposite. When Riad comes back he's carrying the drawings like a file taken out of an old-fashioned metal filing cabinet. He walks slowly and the chickens move out of his way more slowly. He sits opposite me and hands me the drawings one by one. They are drawn with a hard-lead pencil, from memory and with great patience. Stroke upon stroke in the evenings after work, until the blacks become as black as he wants, the greys remaining silvery. They are on quite large sheets of paper.

A drawing of a water pitcher. A drawing of his mother. A drawing of a house which was destroyed, of windows that gave on to rooms which have gone.

When I at last put the drawings down, an older man, with the enduring face of a peasant, addresses me. It sounds as if you know about chickens, he says. When a hen falls ill, she stops laying. Little to be done. One day though, she wakes up and feels Death approaching. One day she realizes she's going to die, and what happens? She begins laying again, and nothing but death can stop her. We are like that hen.

The checkpoints function as interior frontiers imposed on the Occupied territories, yet they do not resemble any normal frontier-post. They are constructed and manned in such a way that everyone who passes is reduced to the status of an unwanted refugee.

Impossible to underestimate the importance for the stranglehold of Decor, used as a constant reminder of who are the victors and who should recognize that they are the conquered. Palestinians have to undergo, often several times a day, the humiliation of playing the part of refugees in their own homeland.

Everyone crossing has to walk on foot past the checkpoint, where soldiers, loaded guns at the ready, pick on whoever they wish to 'check'. No vehicles can cross. The traditional road has been destroyed. The new obligatory 'route' has been strewn with boulders, stones and other minor obstacles. Consequently, all, even the fit, have to hobble across.

The sick and elderly are pushed in wooden boxes on four wheels (boxes originally made for carting vegetables in the market) by young men, who earn a small living like this. They hand each passenger a cushion to soften the bumps. They listen to their stories. They always know the latest news. (The barriers alter every day.) They offer advice, they lament and they are proud of the little aid they offer. They are perhaps the nearest to a Chorus of the tragedy.

Some 'commuters' walk with the aid of a stick, some even on crutches. Everything which normally would be in the boot of a vehicle has to be hoicked across in bundles carried by hand or on the back. The distance of a crossing can change overnight from anything between 300 metres and 1.5 kilometres.

Palestinian couples, except for certain more sophisticated young ones, generally observe in public the decorum of a certain distance. At the checkpoints couples of all ages hold hands as they cross, searching with each step for a foothold, and calculating exactly the right pace for hobbling past the pointing guns, neither too fast – hurrying can arouse suspicion, nor too slow – hesitation can provoke a 'game' for relieving the guards' chronic boredom.

The vindictiveness of many (not all) Israeli soldiers is particular. It has little to do with the cruelty which Euripedes described and lamented, for here the confrontation is not between equals, but between the all-powerful and the apparently powerless. Yet this power of the powerful is accompanied by a furious frustration: the discovery that, despite all their weapons, their power has an inexplicable limit.

I want to change some euros for shekels – the Palestinians have no currency of their own. I walk down the Main Street passing many small shops, and, occasionally, a man sitting on a chair, where there would once have been a pavement before the invasion of the tanks. In their hands these men hold wads of bank notes. I approach a young one and say I want to change 100 euros. (For that amount one could buy in one of the gold shops a small bracelet for a child.) He consults a child's pocket calculator and hands me several hundred shekels.

I walk on. A boy who, age-wise, might be the brother of the girl with the imaginary golden bracelet, holds out some chewing gum for me to buy. He is from one of the two refugee camps in Ramallah. I buy. He's also selling plastic covers for the magnetic ID cards in the wallet. His scowl suggests I buy all the chewing gum. I do.

Half an hour passes and I'm in the vegetable market. A man is selling garlic the size of electric light-bulbs. There are many people close together. Somebody taps me on the shoulder. I turn round. It's the money-changer. I gave you, he says, fifty shekels too little, here they are. I take five notes of ten. You were easy to find, he adds. I thank him.

The expression in his eyes as he looks at me reminds me of an old woman I have seen the day before. An expression of great attention to the moment. Calm and considered, as if it could conceivably be the last moment.

The money-changer then turns and begins his long walk back to the chair.

I met the old woman in the village of Kobar. The house was concrete, unfinished and sparse. On the walls of the bare salon were framed photographs of her nephew, Marwan Barghouti. Marwan as a boy, an adolescent, a man of forty. Today he is in an Israeli prison. If he survives, he is one of the few political leaders of the Fatah with whom it will be essential to consult concerning any solid peace agreement.

Whilst we were drinking lemon juice and the Aunt was making coffee, her grandchildren came out into the garden: two boys aged about seven and nine. The younger one is called Homeland and the elder one Struggle. They ran around in every direction and would suddenly stop, looking intently at one another, as if they were hiding behind something and peering out to see whether the other one had spotted them. Then they would move again to another invisible hide-out. A game they had invented and played together many times.

The third child was four years old. On his face were red and white daubs as on a clown's, and he stood apart like a clown, wistful, jokey, unsure when it would be over. He had chickenpox and knew he should not approach visitors.

When it came to saying good-bye, the Aunt held my hand, and in her eyes, there was this same special expression of attention to the moment.

If two people are laying a tablecloth on a table, they glance at one another to check the placing of the cloth. Imagine the table is the world and the cloth the lives of those we have to save. Such was the expression.

A small brass bowl called a Fear Cup. Engraved with filigree geometric patterns and some verses from the Koran arranged in the form of a flower. Fill it with water and leave it outside under the stars for a night. Then drink the water whilst praying that it will alleviate the pain and cure you.

For many sicknesses the Fear Cup is clearly less effective than a course of antibiotics. But a bowl of water which has reflected the time of the stars, the same water from which every living thing was made, as is said in the Koran, may help to resist the stranglehold . . .

Two weeks after leaving Ramallah I am in Finistere in north-west France, looking out to sea. The contrast of climate and vegetation cannot be greater. The only thing in common is an abundance of brambles – *toot il alliq*. The Finistere coast is green with ferns, until it falls to the rocks. And it is broken into countless small islands by the impact of an ocean, which changes its colour every half hour. The western coast of Europe from Cornwall to Spanish Galicia has been named Land's End. Here the land ends in ferns and islets like boulders.

I have come to see the most ancient built monument in the world, constructed a thousand years before the earliest pyramids. It too was constructed as a funerary monument. What I'm looking at, Eqbal, is a pile of stones. The guide books call it a cairn.

Yet it's far more than a cairn; it's a highly articulated sculpture. Every forty centimetres of it has been, as it were, hand-written. It's over seventy metres long, about twenty-five metres wide and eight or ten metres tall, and in each direction each stone joins the following one intentionally, as if the stones were hand-written words.

Imagine the deck of a ship. She's heading north-east to get out of the bay of Morlaix, and then she can go west towards America. This ship with her Homeric prow (local legend has it that Odysseus passed by this coast on his way to Cork), this ship is made of stones, and naturally she is married to the earth!

According to the carbon datings, she was built at least six thousand years ago, on two separate occasions. First the stern was made with greenish metamorphic dolerite stones, such as abound along the coast with its acid earth beneath the ferns. Then, a century or two later, the prow was added, made mostly with oat-coloured granite, which came from the little island of Sterec.

There was a third construction which may have been a second ship of death, but this was utterly destroyed in the 1950s, when the whole site, which had long since been overgrown and covered with earth, was being exploited as a quarry, and the stones used for making gravel.

Archaeologists deduce that each part of the ship, on the two occasions, was built within a few months. And this, given the labour involved, presumes that a whole settler community of several hundred people worked together on it.

Most of the stones are the size and weight of what a strong man might carry between his two arms. There are also smaller ones, small as a fist, for filling in the recalcitrant spaces left in the otherwise perfect fitting together of the larger ones.

The ship's decks are smooth, not cobbled. And there are a few megaliths, taller than a man, used as lintels over the entrances to passageways, or, sometimes, as a table-roof for vaulted chambers. On the lower deck, twenty-two dry-stone passages, from port and starboard, lead to eleven vaulted cabins, where the dead were placed.

I follow one such passage, which is like a sentence leading to a centre, and here, in the half-destroyed sanctuary, I gaze at the stones corbelling out. They are the same as millions of other stones on the beaches of this coast, except that here, they speak and are eloquent, due to their arrangement.

Chaos perhaps has its reasons, but chaos is dumb. From the human capacity to arrange, to place, come language and communication. The word *place* is both verb and noun. The capacity of arrangement and the capacity to recognize and name a site. Aren't both inseparable in their origin from the human need to respect and defend their dead?

A strange comparison occurs to me. What inspired hundreds of people to work together for several months to build this ship of stones is perhaps quite close to what inspires kids in Palestine to hurl stones at the tanks of an occupying army.

The Chorus in Our Heads
or
Pier Paolo Pasolini

(June 2006)

I F I SAY HE was like an angel, I can't imagine anything more stupid being said about him. An angel painted by Cosimo Tura? No. There's a St. George by Tura which is his speaking likeness! He abhorred official saints and beatific angels. So why say it? Because his habitual and immense sadness allowed him to share jokes, and the look on his distressed face distributed laughter, guessing exactly who needed it most. And the more intimate his touch, the more lucid it became! He could whisper to people softly about the worst that was happening to them and they somehow suffered a little less, '. . . for we never have despair without some small hope.' 'Disperazione senza un po' di speranza.' Pier Paolo Pasolini (1922–1975).

I think he doubted many things about himself, but never his gift of prophesy which was, perhaps, the one thing he would have liked to have doubted. Yet, since he was prophetic, he comes to our aid in what we are living today. I have just watched a film made in 1963. Astonishingly, it was never publicly shown. It arrives like the proverbial message put in a bottle and washed up forty years later on our beach.

At that earlier time, many people followed world events by watching not the TV news, but newsreels in cinemas. In 1962 G. Ferranti, an Italian producer of such reels, had a bright idea. He would give the already notorious Pasolini access to his news archives from 1945–62, in order to answer the question: Why was there everywhere in the world a fear of war? He could edit whatever material he chose, and write a voice-over commentary. The resulting one-hour film would hopefully boost the newsreel company's prestige. The question was 'hot' because, at that moment, the fear of yet another World War was indeed widespread. The nuclear warhead crisis between Cuba, the USA and the USSR erupted in October 1962.

Pasolini, who had already made *Accattone*, *Mamma Roma*, and *La Ricotta*, accepted for his own reasons, because he was in love with and at war with History. He made the film, and entitled it *La Rabbia* (Rage).[1]

When the producers saw it, they got cold feet and insisted that a second filmmaker, a notoriously right-wing journalist called Giovanni Guareschi, should now make a second part and that the two films should then be presented as one. As things turned out, neither was shown.

La Rabbia, I would say, is a film inspired by a fierce sense of endurance, not anger. Pasolini looks at what is happening in the world with unflinching lucidity. (There are angels drawn by Rembrandt who have the same gaze.) And he does so because reality is all we have to love. There's nothing else.

His dismissal of the hypocrisies, half-truths and pretences of the greedy and powerful is total because they breed and foster ignorance, which is a form of blindness towards reality. Also because they shit on memory, including the memory of language itself, which is our first heritage.

Yet the reality he loved could not be simply endorsed, for at that moment it represented a too deep historical disappointment. The ancient hopes which flowered and opened out in 1945, after the defeat of Fascism, had been betrayed.

The USSR had invaded Hungary. France had begun its cowardly war against Algeria. The coming to independence of the former African colonies was a macabre charade. Lumumba had been liquidated by the puppets of the CIA. Neo-capitalism was already planning its global take-over.

Yet despite this, what had been bequeathed was far too precious and too tough to abandon. Or, to put it another way, the unspoken ubiquitous demands of reality were impossible to ignore. The demand in the way a shawl was worn. In a young man's face. In a street full of people demanding less injustice. In the laughter of their expectations and the recklessness of their jokes. From this came his rage of endurance.

Pasolini's answer to the original question was simple: The class struggle explains war.

The film ends with an imaginary soliloquy by Gagarin, after he has seen the planet from outer space, in which he observes that all men, seen from that distance away, are brothers who should renounce the planet's bloody practices.

Essentially, however, the film is about experiences which both the question and answer leave aside. About the coldness of winter for the homeless. About the warmth that the remembering of revolutionary heroes can offer, about the irreconcilability of freedom and hate, about the peasant flair of Pope John XXIII whose eyes smile like a tortoise, about Stalin's faults which were our faults, about the devilish temptation of thinking any struggle is over, about the death of Marilyn Monroe and how beauty is all that remains from the stupidity of the past and the savagery of the future, about how Nature and Wealth are the same thing for the possessing classes, about our mothers and their hereditary tears, about the children of children of children, about the injustices that follow even a noble victory, about the little panic in the eyes of Sophia Loren when she watches a fisherman's hands cutting open an eel . . .

The commentary over the black-and-white film is spoken

by two anonymous voices; in fact the voices of two of his friends: the painter Renato Guttuso and the writer Giorgio Bassani. One is like the voice of an urgent commentator, and the other the voice of someone who is half-historian and half-poet, a soothsayer's voice. Among the major news items covered are the Hungarian revolution of '56, Eisenhower running a second time for President, the coronation of Queen Elizabeth, Castro's victory in Cuba.

The first voice informs us and the second one reminds us. Of what? Not exactly of the forgotten (it is more cunning), but rather of what we have chosen to forget, and such choices often begin in childhood. Pasolini forgot nothing from his childhood – hence the constant coexistence in what he seeks of pain and fun. We are made ashamed of our forgetting.

The two voices function like a Greek chorus. They cannot affect the outcome of what is being shown. They do not interpret. They question, listen, observe and then give voice to what the viewer may, more or less inarticulately, be feeling.

And they achieve this because they are aware that the language being shared by actors, chorus and viewer is the depot of an age-long common experience. The language itself is complicit with our reactions. It cannot be cheated. The voices speak out, not to cap an argument, but because it would be shameful, given the length of human experience and pain, if what they had to say was not said. Should it go unsaid, the capacity for being human would be slightly diminished.

In Ancient Greece the chorus was made up, not of actors, but of male citizens, chosen for that year by the chorus-master, the *choregus*. They represented the city, they came from the *agora*, the forum. Yet as chorus they became the voices of several generations. When they spoke of what the public had already recognized, they were grandparents. When they gave voice to what the public felt but had been unable to articulate, they were the unborn.

All this Pasolini does single-handed with his two voices as he paces, enraged, between the ancient world, which will disappear with the last peasant, and the future world of ferocious calculation.

At several moments the film reminds us of the limits of rational explanation, and of the frequent vulgarity of terms like optimism and pessimism.

The best brains of Europe and the USA, it announces, are theoretically explaining what it means to die (fighting with Castro) in Cuba. Yet what it really means to die in Cuba – or Naples or Seville – can only be told with pity, in the light of a song and in the light of tears.

At another moment it proposes that all of us dream of the right to be like some of our ancestors were! And then adds: Only revolution can save the past.

La Rabbia is a film of love. Yet its lucidity is comparable to that in Kafka's aphorism: 'The Good is, in a certain sense, comfortless.'

This is why I say Pasolini was like an angel.

The film lasts only an hour, an hour that was fashioned, measured, edited forty years ago. And it is in such contrast to the news commentaries we watch and the information fed to us now, that when the hour is over, you tell yourself that it is not only animal and plant species which are being destroyed or made extinct today, but also set after set of our human priorities. The latter are systematically sprayed, not with pesticides, but with ethicides – agents that kill ethics and therefore any notion of history and justice.

Particularly targeted are those of our priorities which have evolved from the human need for sharing, bequeathing, consoling, mourning and hoping. And the ethicides are sprayed day and night by the mass news media.

The ethicides are perhaps less effective, less speedy than the controllers hoped, but they have succeeded in burying and covering up the imaginative space that any central public forum represents and requires. (Our forums are everywhere but for the moment they are marginal.) And on the wasteland of the covered-over forums (reminiscent of the wasteland on which he was assassinated by the Fascists) Pasolini joins us with his Rabbia, and his enduring example of how to carry the chorus in our heads.

A Master of Pitilessness?

(May 2004)

V ISIT THE FRANCIS BACON exhibition at the Maillol
Museum in Paris. Read Susan Sontag's book *Regarding
the Pain of Others*. The exhibition represents succinctly a long
life's work. The book is a remarkably probing meditation about
war, physical mutilation and the effect of war photographs.
Somewhere in my mind the book and exhibition refer to
one another. I'm not yet sure how.

As a figurative painter, Bacon had the cunning of a Fra-
gonard. (The comparison would have amused him, and both
were accomplished painters of physical sensation – one of
pleasure and the other of pain.) Bacon's cunning has understandably intrigued and challenged at least two generations
of painters. If during fifty years I have been critical of Bacon's
work, it is because I was convinced he painted in order to
shock, both himself and others. And such a motive, I
believed, would wear thin with time. Last week, as I walked
backwards and forwards before the paintings in the Rue de

Grenelle, I perceived something I'd not understood before, and I felt a sudden gratitude to a painter whose work I'd questioned for such a long while.

Bacon's vision from the late 1930s to his death in 1992 was of a pitiless world. He repeatedly painted the human body or parts of the body in discomfort or want or agony. Sometimes the pain involved looks as if it has been inflicted, more often it seems to originate from within, from the guts of the body itself, from the misfortune of being physical. Bacon consciously played with his name to create a myth and he succeeded in this. He claimed descent from his namesake, the sixteenth-century English empiricist philosopher, and he painted human flesh as if it were a rasher of bacon.

Yet it is not this which makes his world more pitiless than any painted before. European art is full of assassinations, executions and martyrs. In Goya, the first artist of the twentieth-century (twentieth, yes), one listens to the artist's own outrage. What is different in Bacon's vision is that there are no witnesses and there is no grief. Nobody painted by him notices what is happening to somebody else painted by him. Such ubiquitous indifference is crueller than any mutilation.

In addition there is the muteness of the settings in which he places his figures. This muteness is like the coldness of a freezer, which remains constant whatever is deposited in it. Bacon's theatre, unlike Artaud's, has little to do with ritual, because no space around his figures receives their gestures. Every enacted calamity is presented as a mere collateral accident.

During his lifetime such a vision was nourished and haunted by the melodramas of a very provincial bohemian circle, within which nobody gave a fuck about what was happening elsewhere. And yet . . . and yet the pitiless world Bacon conjured up and tried to exorcise has turned out to be prophetic. It can happen that the personal drama of an artist reflects within half a century the crisis of an entire civilization. How? Mysteriously.

Has not the world always been pitiless? Today's pitilessness is perhaps more unremitting, pervasive and continuous. It spares neither the planet itself nor anyone living on it anywhere. Abstract because deriving from the sole logic of the pursuit of profit (as cold as the freezer), it threatens to make obsolete all other sets of belief, along with their traditions of facing the cruelty of life with dignity and some flashes of hope.

Return to Bacon and what his work reveals. He obsessively used the pictorial language and thematic references of some earlier painters – such as Velázquez, Michelangelo, Ingres or Van Gogh. This 'continuity' makes the devastation of his vision more complete.

The Renaissance idealization of the naked human body, the Church's promise of redemption, the Classical notion of heroism, or Van Gogh's ardent nineteenth-century belief in democracy are revealed within his vision to be in tatters, powerless before the pitilessness. Bacon picks up the shreds and uses them as swabs. This is what I had not taken in before. Here was the revelation.

A revelation which confirms an insight: to engage today

with the traditional vocabulary, as employed by the powerful and their media, only adds to the surrounding murkiness and devastation. This does not necessarily mean silence. It means choosing the voices one wishes to join.

The present period of history is one of the Wall. When the Berlin one fell, the prepared plans to build walls everywhere were unrolled. Concrete, bureaucratic, surveillance, security, racist walls. Everywhere the walls separate the desperate poor from those who hope against hope to stay relatively rich. The walls cross every sphere, from crop cultivation to health care. They exist too in the richest metropolises of the world. The Wall is the front line of what, long ago, was called the Class War.

On the one side: every armament conceivable, the dream of no-body-bag wars, the media, plenty, hygiene, many passwords to glamour. On the other: stones, short supplies, feuds, the violence of revenge, rampant illness, an acceptance of death and an ongoing preoccupation with surviving one more night – or perhaps one more week – together.

The choice of meaning in the world today is here between the two sides of the wall. The wall is also inside each one of us. Whatever our circumstances, we can choose within ourselves which side of the wall we are attuned to. It is not a wall between good and evil. Both exist on both sides. The choice is between self-respect and self-chaos.

On the side of the powerful there is a conformism of fear – they never forget the Wall – and the mouthing of words which no longer mean anything. Such muteness is what Bacon painted.

On the other side there are multitudinous, disparate, sometimes disappearing, languages, with whose vocabularies a sense can be made of life, even if, particularly if, that sense is tragic.

> When my words were wheat
> I was earth.
> When my words were anger
> I was storm.
> When my words were rock
> I was river.
> When my words turned honey
> Flies covered my lips.[1]

Mahmoud Darweesh

Bacon painted the muteness fearlessly, and in this was he not closer to those on the other side, for whom the walls are one more obstacle to get around? It could be . . .

Ten Dispatches About Endurance
in Face of Walls

(October 2004)

1

The wind got up in
the night and took our plans away.

(Chinese proverb)

2

The poor have no residence. They have homes because they
remember mothers or grandfathers or an aunt who brought
them up. A residence is a fortress, not a story; it keeps the
wild at bay. A residence needs walls. Nearly everyone among
the poor dreams of a small residence, like dreaming of rest.
However great the congestion, the poor live in the open,
where they improvise, not residences, but places for themselves. These places are as much protagonists as their
occupants; the places have their own lives to live and do

not, like residences, wait on others. The poor live with the wind, with dampness, flying dust, silence, unbearable noise (sometimes with both; yes, that's possible), with ants, with large animals, with smells coming from the earth, rats, smoke, rain, vibrations from elsewhere, rumours, nightfall and with each other. Between the inhabitants and these presences there are no clear marking lines. Inextricably confounded, they together make up the place's life.

'Twilight was setting in; the sky, wrapped in cool grey fog, was already being closed off by darkness; and the wind, after spending the day rustling stubble and bare bushes that had gone dead in preparation for winter, now lays itself down in still low places on the earth . . .'[1]

The poor are collectively unseizable. They are not only the majority on the planet, they are everywhere and the smallest event speaks of them. This is why the essential activity of the rich today is the building of walls – walls of concrete, of electronic surveillance, of missile barrages, minefields, frontier controls, and opaque media screens.

3

The lives of the poor are mostly grief, interrupted by moments of illumination. Each life has its own propensity for illumination and no two are the same. (Conformism is a habit cultivated by the well-off.) Illuminated moments arrive by way of tenderness and love – the consolation of being recognized and needed and embraced for being what one suddenly is! Other moments are illuminated by an intuition, despite everything, that the human species serves for something.

'Nazar, tell me something or other – something more important than anything.'

Aidym turned down the wick in the lamp in order to use less paraffin. She understood that, since there was something or other in life that was more important than anything, it was essential to take care of every good that there was.

'I don't know the thing that really matters, Aidym,' said Chagataev. 'I haven't thought about it, I've never had time. But if we've both of us been born, then there must be something in us that really matters.'

Aidym agreed: 'A little that does matter . . . and a lot that doesn't.'

Aidym prepared supper. She took a flat bread out of a sack, spread it with sheep's fat and broke it in half. She gave Chagataev the big half, and took the small half herself. They silently chewed their food by the weak light of the lamp. In the Ust-Yurt and the desert it was quiet, uncertain and dark.[2]

4

From time to time despair enters into the lives which are mostly grief. Despair is the emotion which follows a sense of betrayal. A hope against hope (which is still far from a promise) collapses or is collapsed; despair fills the space in the soul which was occupied by that hope. Despair has nothing to do with nihilism.

Nihilism, in its contemporary sense, is the refusal to

believe in any scale of priorities beyond the pursuit of profit, considered as the end-all of social activity, so that, precisely: everything has its price. Nihilism is resignation before the contention that Price is all. It is the most current form of human cowardice. But not one to which the poor often succumb.

'He began to pity his body and his bones; his mother had once gathered them together for him from the poverty of her flesh – not because of love and passion, not for pleasure, but out of the most everyday necessity. He felt as if he belonged to others, as if he were the last possession of those who have no possessions, about to be squandered to no purpose, and he was seized by the greatest, most vital fury of his life.'[3]

[A word of explanation about these quotations. They are from the stories of the great Russian writer, Andrei Platonov (1899–1951), wonderfully translated by Robert Chandler. Platonov wrote about the poverty which occurred during the Civil War and later during the forced collectivization of Soviet agriculture in the early 1930s. What made this poverty unlike more ancient poverties was the fact that its desolation contained shattered hopes. It fell to the ground exhausted, it got to its feet, it staggered, it marched on amongst shards of betrayed promises and smashed words. Platonov often used the term *dushevny bednyak*, which means literally 'poor souls'. It referred to those from whom everything had been taken so that the emptiness within them was immense and in that immensity only their soul was left – that's to say their ability to feel and suffer. His stories do not add to the grief being lived, they save something. 'Out of our ugliness will grow the world's heart,' he wrote in the early 1920s.

The world today is suffering another form of modern poverty. No need to quote the figures; they are widely known and repeating them again only makes another wall of statistics. More than half the world population live with less than $2 a day. Local cultures, with their partial remedies – both physical and spiritual – for some of life's afflictions, are being systematically destroyed or attacked. The new technology and means of communication, the free-market economy, productive abundance, parliamentary democracy, are failing, so far as the poor are concerned, to keep any of their promises beyond that of the supply of certain cheap consumerist goods, which the poor can buy when they steal.

Platonov understood living modern poverty more deeply than any other storyteller I have come across.]

5

The secret of storytelling amongst the poor is the conviction that stories are told so that they may be listened to elsewhere, where somebody, or perhaps a legion of people, knows better than the storyteller or the story's protagonists what life means. The powerful can't tell stories: boasts are the opposite of stories, and any story, however mild, has to be fearless; the powerful today live nervously.

A story refers life to an alternative and more final judge who is far away. Maybe the judge is located in the future, or in the past that is still attentive, or maybe somewhere over the hill, where the day's luck has changed (the poor have to refer often to bad or good luck) so that the last have become first.

Story-time (the time within a story) is not linear. The living and the dead meet as listeners and judges within this time, and the greater the number of listeners felt to be there, the more *intimate* the story becomes to each listener. Stories are one way of sharing the belief that justice is imminent. And for such a belief, children, women and men will fight at a given moment with astounding ferocity. This is why tyrants fear storytelling: all stories somehow refer to the story of their fall.

'Wherever he went, he only had to promise to tell a story and people would take him in for the night: a story's stronger than a Tsar. There was just one thing: if he began telling stories before the evening meal, no-one ever felt hungry and he didn't get anything to eat. So the old soldier always asked for a bowl of soup first.'[4]

6

The worst cruelties of life are its killing injustices. Almost all promises are broken. The poor's acceptance of adversity is neither passive nor resigned. It's an acceptance which peers behind the adversity and discovers there something nameless. Not a promise, for (almost) all promises are broken; rather something like a bracket, a parenthesis in the otherwise remorseless flow of history. And the sum total of these parentheses is eternity.

This can be put the other way round: on this earth there is no happiness without a longing for justice.

Happiness is not something to be pursued, it is something met, an encounter. Most encounters, however, have a sequel; this is their promise. The encounter with happiness has no sequel. All is there instantly. Happiness is what pierces grief.

'"We thought there was nothing left in the world, that everything had disappeared long ago. And if we were the only ones left, what was the point of living?"

'"We went to check," said Allah. "Were there any other people anywhere? We wanted to know."

'Chagataev understood them and asked if this meant they were now convinced about life and wouldn't be dying any more.

'"Dying's no use," said Cherkezov. "To die once – now you might think that's something necessary and useful. But dying once doesn't help you to understand your own happiness – and no one gets the chance to die twice. So dying gets you nowhere."'[5]

7

'Whilst the rich drank tea and ate mutton, the poor were waiting for the warmth and for the plants to grow.'[6]

The difference between seasons, as also the difference between night and day, shine and rain, is vital. The flow of time is turbulent. The turbulence makes lifetimes shorter – both in fact and subjectively. Duration is brief. Nothing lasts. This is as much a prayer as a lament.

'(The mother) was grieving that she had died and forced her children to mourn for her; if she could have, she would have gone on living forever so that nobody should suffer on her account, or waste, on her account, the heart and the body to which she had given birth . . . but the mother had not been able to stand living for very long.'[7]

Death occurs when life has no scrap left to defend.

8

'. . . it was as if she were alone in the world, free from happiness and sorrow, and she wanted to dance a little, right away, to listen to music, to hold hands with other people . . .'[8]

They are accustomed to living in close proximity with one another, and this creates its own spatial sense; space is not so much an emptiness as an exchange. When people are living on top of one another, any action taken by one has repercussions on the others. Immediate physical repercussions. Every child learns this.

There is a ceaseless spatial negotiation which may be considerate or cruel, conciliating or dominating, unthinking or calculated, but which recognizes that an exchange is not something abstract but a physical accommodation. Their elaborate sign languages of gestures and hands are an expression of such physical sharing. Outside the walls collaboration is as natural as fighting; scams are current and intrigue, which depends upon taking a distance, is rare.

The word 'private' has a totally different ring on the two sides of the wall. On one side it denotes property; on the other an acknowledgement of the temporary need of someone to be left, as if alone, for a while.

The space of choices is also limited. The poor choose as much as the rich, perhaps more, for each choice is starker.

There are no colour charts which offer a choice between 170 different shades. The choice is close-up – between this or that. Often it is made vehemently, for it entails the refusal of what has not been chosen. Each choice is quite close to a sacrifice. And the sum of the choices is a person's destiny.

9

No development (the word has a capital D, as an article of faith, on the other side of the wall), no insurance. Neither an open future nor an assured future exist. The future is not awaited. Yet there is continuity; generation is linked to generation. Hence a respect for age, since the old are a proof of this continuity – or even a demonstration that once, long ago, a future existed. Children are the future. The future is the ceaseless struggle to see that they have enough to eat and the sometimes-chance of their learning with education what the parents never learnt.

'When they finished talking, they threw their arms around each other. They wanted to be happy right away, now, sooner than their future and zealous work would bring results in personal and in general happiness. The heart brooks no delay, it sickens, as if believing in nothing.'[9]

Here the future's unique gift is desire. The future induces the spurt of desire towards itself. The young are more flagrantly young than on the other side of the wall. The gift appears as a gift of nature in all its urgency and supreme assurance. Religious and community laws still apply. Indeed, amongst the chaos, which is more apparent than real, these laws become real. Yet the silent desire for procreation is incontestable and overwhelming. It is the same desire that will forage for food for the children and then seek, sooner or later (best sooner), the consolation of fucking again. This is the future's gift.

10

The multitudes have answers to questions which have not yet been posed, and they have the capacity to outlive the walls.

The questions are not yet asked because to do so requires words and concepts which ring true, and those currently being used to name events have been rendered meaningless: Democracy, Liberty, Productivity, etc.

With new concepts the questions will soon be posed, for history involves precisely such a process of questioning. Soon? Within a generation.

Meanwhile, the answers abound in the multitudes' multiple ingenuities for getting by, their refusal of frontiers, their search for holes in the walls, their adoration of children, their readiness when necessary to become martyrs, their belief in continuity, their recurring acknowledgement that life's gifts are small and priceless.

Trace with a finger tonight her (his) hairline before sleep.

Flesh and Speeches

(July 2005)

EVERYONE WAS STUNNED. We could see a flickering light and thought there was going to be a fire. We could not open the door of the carriage at first; when we got out, we could see seriously injured people in the tunnel.' These are the words of Loyita Worley, a passenger on the Circle Line train going to Aldgate, a little before 9 a.m. on Thursday, 7 July.

People underground are both sheltered and helpless. Tunnels are ways of escape and terrible traps. The dust suffocates when the tunnels are blocked.

To blow to pieces those going to their early morning work by public transport is to attack, in shameful stealth, the defenceless. The victims suffer more pain and for far, far longer than the suicide-bomber. And such suffering gives them most surely the right to judge.

Yet others, the politicians, rush in (from Gleneagles to

London) to speak in their name, whilst serving their own interests, which involve gross simplifications, the use of terms that deliberately confuse and, above all, an attempt to justify themselves and their past – however disastrous the errors committed.

Not even the innocence of the pain and grief they have come to staunch and console appear to give them pause, so that for one moment they hesitate.

'I kept closing my eyes and thinking of outside. It was frightening because all the lights had gone out and we didn't hear anything from the driver, so we wondered how he was.' (Fiona Trueman – on the Piccadilly Line)

The calm of Londoners, who suffered the outrage of the explosions and the ordeal of waiting for news from dear ones who may have been there (that silence which cuts like a blade between the two lobes of your heart), impressed the watching world, as did the calm of Madrid's population the previous year. Such calm could hopefully encourage clear and, above all, precise thinking. In Spain circumstances allowed it to do so, and one of the first acts of the newly elected government was to withdraw Spanish troops from the war in Iraq, a war which the majority of Spaniards were vehemently opposed to.

In London, despite the evident failure of that war to bring anything but chaos and ruin to the nation it claimed to be liberating, the effect of the atrocities suffered by people on their modest way to work has only been to increase the intransigence of the prime minister and government, who tugged a protesting country into an unnecessary war.

On the morning of the explosions, speaking from Downing Street, Blair declared: '[Terrorists] are trying to use the slaughter of innocent people to cow us, to frighten us out of doing the things that we want to do, trying to stop us going about our business . . .'

Those who argue that Al Qaeda was active before the invasion of Iraq, and that therefore the fighting in Baghdad or Fallujah is irrelevant to the London bombings, are arguing in bad faith. The same bad faith which encouraged them to lie about the weapons of mass destruction which did not exist. Bin Laden was certainly planning his attacks against the West before the Iraqi war, but that war, and what was and is happening there, is supplying Al Qaeda with a steady flow of new recruits. Eliza Manningham-Buller, head of MI5, is said to have warned other G8 countries about the danger 'of a new generation of fanatics as a result of the war in Iraq.' And she, one can assume, knows what she is talking about.

The atrocities were planned to coincide with the 2005 G8 meeting, at which the British prime minister was President. What happened at that meeting is not another story but another part of the same one. In this context it is not the Koran that should be studied, but the behaviour of the richest countries and corporations in the world. Those corporations consistently wage their own 'jihad' against any target that opposes the maximization of their profits.

The war in Iraq was conveniently removed from this year's G8 agenda. The agreed priority was to reach some agreement about action in face of the disastrous overheating of the planet, and Africa's poverty.

Before the meeting, voices from all over the world – economists, rock singers, ecologists, musicians, religious leaders – appealed, in the name of conscience and solidarity, for new and unprecedented decisions, for some change that might improve the planet's future chances. And what happened? After you've sorted through the rhetoric, like a rag-picker: almost nothing. A little dance of statistics. But at the flat rate of the rag-pickers – nothing. Why?

Fanaticism comes from any form of chosen blindness accompanying the pursuit of a single dogma. The G8's dogma is that the making of profit has to be mankind's guiding principle, before which everything else from the traditional past or aspiring future must be sacrificed as illusion.

The so-called war against terrorism is in fact a war between two fanaticisms.

To bracket the two together seems outrageous. One is theocratic, the other positivist and secular. One is the fervent belief of a defensive minority, the other the unquestioned assumption of an amorphous, confident elite. One sets out to kill, the other plunders, leaves and lets die. One is strict, the other lax. One brooks no argument, the other 'communicates' and tries to 'spin' into every corner of the world. One claims the right to spill innocent blood, the other the right to sell the entire earth's water. Outrageous to compare them!

Yet the *outrage* of what happened in London on the Piccadilly line, the Circle line and the No. 30 bus was the misadventure of many thousands of vulnerable people, struggling to survive and make some sense of their lives, being inadvertently caught in the global crossfire of those two fanaticisms.

The poet Keats wrote: 'Fanatics have their dreams wherewith they weave a paradise for a sect.' All those who belong to no sect would choose to live, not in a paradise, but above ground, together.

About Disconnecting

(September 2005)

S OMETIMES IT HAPPENS that a question is for a moment more pertinent than answers or explanations. I'm not sure that the question I want to ask is of this order, for it has the air of being naive. Nevertheless I'll share it with you.

During the month of September, as a consequence of the catastrophe that occurred in New Orleans whose effects and pain will continue for years, people in the USA and throughout the world have started to re-examine the record of Bush, Cheney, Rumsfeld, Rice, Rove et al., who are the present leaders of the first world superpower.

A shift in opinion has taken place almost overnight. History, throwing us all back into our seats, suddenly opened its throttle. Whilst at the same time in New Orleans 20,000 people were desperately stranded and trapped in the Superdome.

Katrina – everyone refers to the hurricane by her name,

as if she were some kind of avatar – revealed that there is dire and increasing poverty in the US, that blacks are typically treated as unwanted second-class citizens, that the systematic cutting of government investment in public institutions has produced widespread social disequilibrium and destitution (40 million Americans live without any aid if they fall ill or are hurt), that the so-called war against terrorism is creating administrative chaos, and that within and against all this, voices of protest are being raised loud and clear.

All this, though, was evident before Katrina to those living it, and to those who wanted to know. What she changed was that the media were there for once, showing what was actually happening, and the fury of those to whom it was happening. With her terrible gesture she wiped for a little while the opaque screens clean.

In some gnomic way the as yet innumerable dead on the Gulf Coast spoke not for, but with, the hundred thousand Iraqis who have died as a consequence of the ongoing disastrous and criminal war. Time and again in the US press Katrina and Iraq are being mentioned together. Yet Katrina was regular. She belonged to the familiar weather conditions which affect the Mexican Gulf. She was not hiding in Afghanistan. And merciless as she was, she did not belong to any Axis of Evil. She was simply a natural threat to American lives and property and she was heading for Louisiana.

It was in the self-interest (as well as the national interest) of the President and his chosen colleagues to meet the challenge she threw down, to foresee the needs of her victims and to reduce the ensuing pain and panic to the minimum possible. If they, the government, happened to fail to do this, they would be able to blame nobody else, and they themselves would be blamed. A child could foresee this. And they failed utterly. Their failure was technical, political and emotional. 'Stuff happens,' murmurs Donald Rumsfeld.

Is it possible that this administration is mad? This is my naive question. Wait. Let us try to define the variant of madness, for it may be that it has never occurred before. It has very little to do, for example, with Nero when he fiddled whilst Rome burnt. Any madness, however, implies a severe disconnection with reality, or, to put it more precisely, with the existent.

The variant we are considering touches upon the relationship between fear and confidence, between being threatened and being supreme. There is no negotiation between the two. Their 'madness' operates like a switch which instantly turns one off and the other on. And what is grave about this is that it is in the long periods of negotiating between fear and confidence that the existent is normally surveyed and observed in its multitudinous complexity. It is there one learns about what one is facing. A binary 'madness' excludes this.

On the aircraft carrier *Abraham Lincoln* President Bush announced two years ago: Mission accomplished in Iraq!

In some ways this binary affliction echoes the mechanism of a stock market, wherein there is only buying or selling and the two poles of bull and bear, and the rest of what exists, and how and where, barely impinges.

On Wall Street, the financial analysts are predicting increased profits for the Texan oil corporations as a result of the petrol shortages caused by the Gulf catastrophe.

Five days after Katrina had struck, when President Bush finally visited the devastated city, he astounded journalists by saying: 'I don't think anyone anticipated the breach of the levees.'

On the same day, in the wrecked small town of Biloxi, the President's flying visit was preceded by a team who quickly cleared the rubble and corpses from the route his cortege would take. Two hours later the team vanished, leaving everything else in the town exactly as it was. The rest of what exists barely impinges.

To consider this heartless or cynical is to miss the diagnosis. His visits were a planned operation serving as a prelude to the assertion that: 'We'll once again show the world that the worst adversities bring out the best in America.' Switch turned.

The calculations of the present US government are closely related to the global interests of the corporations and what has been termed the survival of the richest, who today also vacillate constantly and abruptly between fear and confidence.

The economist Grover Norquist, who is a talking head for corporate interests and to whom Bush and Co. listened when planning their tax reforms for the benefit of the rich, is on record as saying: 'I don't want to abolish government. I simply want to reduce it to the size where I can drag it into the bathroom and drown it in the bathtub.'

An ignorance about most of what exists, and an abdication from the very minimum of what can be expected of government – are we not approaching disconnections which amount to what can be called madness when found in the minds of those who believe they can rule the planet?

All political leaders sometimes parry with the truth, but here the disconnections are systematic and crop up not only in their announcements but in their every strategic calculation. Hence their ineptness. Their operation in Afghanistan failed, their war in Iraq has been won (as the saying goes) by Iran, Katrina was allowed to produce the worst natural disaster in US history and terrorist activities are increasing.

On my mobile I received a text message from Orange. It proposed that if I wanted to help the homeless and stranded in Louisiana, I could tap in the word FLOOD to a given number, and the equivalent of five dollars, debited to my account, would immediately be transferred to an aid organization.

I'd like to tap in now some more words to be sent between all of us: HOW MUCH LONGER GLOBAL POWER IN D NUMB HAND OF DOSE WHO KNOW NUTHIN?

Ten Dispatches About Place

(June 2005)

1

SOMEBODY ENQUIRES: ARE YOU still a Marxist? Never before has the devastation caused by the pursuit of profit, as defined by capitalism, been more extensive than it is today. Almost everybody knows this. How then is it possible not to heed Marx who prophesied and analyzed the devastation? The answer might be that people, many people, have lost all their political bearings. Mapless, they do not know where they are heading.

2

Every day people follow signs pointing to some place which is not their home but a chosen destination. Road signs, airport embarkment signs, terminal signs. Some are making their journeys for pleasure, others on business, many out of loss or despair. On arrival they come to realize they are not in the place indicated by the signs they followed. Where they now find themselves has the correct latitude, longitude, local time, currency, yet it does not have the specific gravity of the destination they chose.

They are beside the place they chose to come to. The distance which separates them from it is incalculable. Maybe it's only the width of a thoroughfare, maybe it's a world away. The place has lost what made it a destination. It has lost its territory of experience.

Sometimes a few of these travellers undertake a private journey and find the place they wished to reach, which is often harsher than they foresaw, although they discover it with boundless relief. Many never make it. They accept the signs they follow and it's as if they don't travel, as if they always remain where they already are.

3

Month by month, millions leave their homelands. They leave because there is nothing there, except their *everything*, which does not offer enough to feed their children. Once it did. This is the poverty of the new capitalism.

After long and terrible journeys, after they have experienced the baseness of which others are capable, after they have come to trust their own incomparable and dogged courage, emigrants find themselves waiting on some foreign transit station, and then all they have left of their home continent is *themselves*: their hands, their eyes, their feet, shoulders, bodies, what they wear and what they pull over their heads at night to sleep under, wanting a roof.

In some photos taken in the Red Cross shelter for refugees

and emigrants at Sangatte (near Calais) by Anabell Guerrero we can take account of how a man's fingers are all that remain of a plot of tilled earth, his palms what remain of some riverbed, and how his eyes are a family gathering he will not attend.

4

'I'm going down the stairs in an underground station to take the B line. Crowded here. Where are you? Really! What's the weather like? Getting into the train – call you later . . .'

Of the billions of mobile telephone conversations taking place every hour in the world's cities and suburbs, most, whether they are private or business calls, begin with a statement about the caller's whereabouts. People need straightaway to pinpoint where they are. It is as if they are pursued by doubts suggesting that they may be nowhere. Surrounded by so many abstractions, they have to invent and share their own transient landmarks.

More than thirty years ago, Guy Debord prophetically wrote: '. . . the accumulation of mass-produced commodities for the abstract space of the market, just as it has smashed all regional and legal barriers, and all corporate restrictions of the Middle Ages that maintained the quality of artisanal production, has also destroyed the autonomy and quality of places.'

The key term of the present global chaos is de- or re-localization. This does not only refer to the practice of moving production to wherever labour is cheapest and regulations minimal. It also contains the offshore demented dream of the new ongoing power: the dream of undermining the status and confidence of all previous fixed places, so that the entire world becomes a single fluid market.

The consumer is essentially somebody who feels, or is made to feel, lost, unless he or she is consuming. Brand names and logos become the place names of the Nowhere.

In the past a common tactic employed by those defending their homeland against invaders was to change the road signs so that the one indicating ZARAGOZA pointed in the opposite direction towards BURGOS. Today it is not defenders but foreign invaders who switch signs to confuse local populations, confuse them about who is governing who, the nature of happiness, the extent of grief, or where eternity is to be found. And the aim of all these misdirections is to persuade people that being a client is the ultimate salvation.

Yet clients are defined by where they check out and pay, not by where they live and die.

5

Extensive areas which were once rural places are being turned into zones. The details of the process vary according to the continent – Africa or Central America or Southeast Asia. The initial dismembering, however, always comes from elsewhere and from corporate interests pursuing their appetite for ever more accumulation, which means seizing natural resources (fish in Lake Victoria, wood in the Amazon, petrol wherever it is to be found, uranium in Gabon, etc.), regardless of to whom the land or water belongs. The ensuing exploitation soon demands airports, military and paramilitary bases to defend what is being syphoned off, and collaboration with the local mafiosi. Tribal war, famine and genocide may follow.

People in such zones lose all sense of residence: children become orphans (even when they are not), women become slaves, men desperadoes. Once this has happened, to restore any sense of domesticity takes generations. Each year of such accumulation prolongs the Nowhere in time and space.

6

Meanwhile – and political resistance often begins in a mean-while – the most important thing to grasp and remember is that those who profit from the present chaos, with their embedded commentators in the media, continuously misinform and misdirect. Their declarations will get nobody anywhere.

Yet, at the same time, the information technology developed by the corporations and their armies so they could dominate their Nowhere more speedily is being used by others as a means of communication throughout the Everywhere they are struggling towards.

The Caribbean writer Edouard Glissant puts this very well: '. . . the way to resist globalization is not to deny globality, but to imagine what is the finite sum of all possible particularities and to get used to the idea that, as long as a single particularity is missing, globality will not be what it should be for us.'

We are establishing our own landmarks, naming places, finding poetry. Yes, in the Meanwhile poetry is to be found. Gareth Evans:

> as the brick of the afternoon stores the rose heat of
> the journey
>
> as the rose buds a green room to breathe
> and blossoms like the wind
>
> as the thinning birches whisper their silver stories of
> the wind to the urgent
> in the trucks
>
> as the leaves of the hedge store the light
> that the moment thought it had lost
>
> as the nest of her wrist beats like the chest of a wren
> in the turning air
>
> as the chorus of the earth find their eyes in the sky
> and unwrap them to each other in the teeming dark
>
> *hold everything dear*

7

Their Nowhere generates a strange, because unprecedented, awareness of time. Digital time. It continues for ever uninterrupted through day and night, the seasons, birth and death. As indifferent as money. Yet, although continuous, it is utterly single. It is the time of the present kept apart from the past and future. Within it only the present is weight-bearing, the other two lack gravity. Time is no longer a colonnade, but a single column of ones and zeros. A vertical time with nothing surrounding it, except absence.

Read a few pages of Emily Dickinson and then go and see Von Trier's film *Dogville*. In Dickinson's poetry the presence of the eternal is attendant in every pause. The film, by contrast, remorselessly shows what happens when any trace of the eternal is erased from daily life. What happens is that all words and their entire language are rendered meaningless.

Within a single present, within digital time, no whereabouts can be found or established.

8

Let's take our bearings within another time-set. The eternal, according to Spinoza, is *now*. It is not something awaiting us, but something we encounter during those brief yet timeless moments when everything accommodates everything and no exchange is inadequate.

In her urgent book, *Hope in the Dark*, Rebecca Solnit quotes the Sandinista poet Gioconda Belli describing the moment when they overthrew the Somoza dictatorship in Nicaragua: 'two days that felt as if a magical, age-old spell had been cast over us, taking us back to Genesis, to the very site of the creation of the world.' The fact that the US and its mercenaries later destroyed the Sandinistas in no way diminishes that moment existing in the past, present and future.

9

A kilometre down the road from where I'm writing, there is a field in which four burros graze, two mares and two foals. They are a particularly small species. The black-bordered ears of the mares when they prick them come up to my chin. The foals, only a few weeks old, are the size of large terrier dogs, with the difference that their heads are almost as large as their sides.

I climb over the fence and sit in the field with my back against the trunk of an apple tree. They have made their own tracks across the field and some pass under very low branches where I would have to stoop double. They watch me. There are two areas where there is no grass at all, just reddish earth, and it is to one of these rings that they come many times a day to roll on their backs. Mare first, then foal. The foals already have their black stripe across their shoulders.

Now they approach me. They smell of donkey and bran – not the smell of horses, more discreet. The mares touch the top of my head with their lower jaws. Their muzzles are white. Around their eyes are flies, far more agitated than their own questioning glances.

When they stand in the shade by the edge of the wood the flies go away, and they can stand there almost motionless for half an hour. In the shade at midday time slows down. When one of the foals suckles (ass's milk is the closest to human milk), the mare's ears lie right back and point to her tail.

Surrounded by the four of them in the sunlight, my attention fixes on their legs, all sixteen of them. Their slenderness, their sheerness, their containment of concentration, their surety. (Horses' legs look hysterical by comparison.) Theirs are legs for crossing mountains no horse could tackle, legs for carrying loads which are unimaginable if one considers only the knees, the shanks, the fetlocks, the hocks, the cannon-bones, the pastern-joints, the hooves! Donkeys' legs.

They wander away, heads down, grazing, their ears missing nothing; I watch them, eyes skinned. In our exchanges, such as they are, in the midday company we offer one another, there is a substratum of what I can only describe as gratitude. Four burros in a field, month of June, year 2005.

10

Yes, I'm still amongst other things a Marxist.

Another Side of Desire

(June 2002)

I found an island in your arms,

                  a country in your eyes,

arms that chain, eyes that lie.

Break on through to the other side.

                                    Jim Morrison

D ESIRE. EROTIC DESIRE. The adjective *erotic* is better than *sexual*, for it is less reductionist.

When desire is reciprocal (between two), the notions of lust, or even libido, become out-dated, for they, by definition, are singular, and not double.

The initial energy of such desire comes of course from the biological need to reproduce. Desire is also an invitation to, and a hope for, imagined pleasures. What begins as erotic desire can be swiftly translated into the desire to have and to possess. The social content of desire is indeed *possession*, which is why in the theatre unchecked desire is never far from conflict and tragedy.

The potential force of desire is proverbial in all cultures. Perhaps because an awareness of being desired bestows a unique sense of invulnerability, and when this sense is multiplied by two almost anything can be risked.

Desire begins early and continues late. It can occur at all ages between, say, five and eighty. Age may affect the priorities within desire. Yet these priorities are never standard or uniform. Any desire consists of a multitude of offers and wishes, and, finally, there may be as many varieties of desire as there are erotic encounters.

There are nevertheless common ingredients, and what I call another side of desire is, I believe, present in all desire, although the degree of its importance, its recognizability, may vary. In consumer societies this ingredient is seldom acknowledged publicly, except in rock music, where it is often central.

> There will always be suffering
> It flows through life like water
> I put my hand over hers
> Down in the lime-tree arbour.
>
> Nick Cave

Desire, when reciprocal, is a plot, hatched by two, in the face of, or in defiance of, all the other plots which determine the world. It is a conspiracy of two.

The plan is to offer to the other a reprieve from the pain

of the world. Not happiness (!) but a physical reprieve from the body's huge liability towards pain.

Within all desire there is pity as well as appetite; the two, whatever their relative proportion, are threaded together. Desire is inconceivable without a wound.

If there were any unwounded in this world, they would live without desire.

The conspiracy is to create together a place, a *locus*, of exemption, and the exemption, necessarily temporary, is from the unmitigated hurt which flesh is heir to.

The human body has prowess, grace, playfulness, dignity, and countless other capacities, but it is also intrinsically tragic – as is no animal's body. (No animal is naked.) Desire longs to shield the desired body from the tragic it embodies, and what is more it believes it can. This is its faith.

There is naturally no altruism in desire. The offer of shielding, of conferring exemption, is made through the offer of the whole self, both physical and imaginative. From the start, two bodies are involved, and so the exemption, when and if achieved, covers both.

The exemption is bound to be brief and yet it promises all. The exemption abolishes brevity – and along with it the hurts associated with the threat of the brief.

Observed by a third person, desire is a short parenthesis; experienced from within, it is a transcendence. In both cases, however, day-to-day life continues around, before and after it.

Desire promises exemption. Yet an exemption from the existing natural order is tantamount to disappearance. And this is precisely what desire, at its most ecstatic, proposes: let's vanish.

> Pendant que la marée monte
> (et) que chacun refait ses comptes
> J'emmène au creux de mon ombre
> Des poussières de toi.
> Le vent les portera
> Tout disparaîtra mais
> Le vent nous portera.
>
> Noir Désir

The lovers' disappearance cannot be counted as an evasion, a flight; it is, rather, a shift elsewhere: an entrance into a plenitude. Plenitude is usually thought of as an amassing. Desire insists that it is a giving away: the plenitude of a silence, a darkness in which everything's at peace. Somehow I think of the ancient dream, the legend of the Golden Fleece. (It granted an exemption from a sacrifice.) Symbolically it represents both innocence and wisdom. It lies stretched out in its hiding place, curly, inviolate, complete, worn by nobody.

Once shared and experienced, the exemption which no longer exempts remains unforgettable, and the disappearances still seem more true, more precise than what is apparent and legible.

The sirens wail down the street. As long as you are in my arms, no harm will come to you.

Looking Carefully –
Two Women Photographers

(2005–2006)

1

Ahlam Shibli

(Born in the village of Arab al Shibli, Galilee. 1970.)

F IRST, A DISTINCTION between being simple and simplifying. The former has something to do with reducing or being reduced to the essential. And the latter – simplification – is usually part of a manoeuvre in some struggle for power. Simplifications are self-serving. Most political leaders simplify, whilst the powerless react simply to what is happening. There is often an abyss between the two.

Now let's look at Ahlam Shibli's photographs without making simplifications. They offer, amongst other things, a political lesson and are, in this sense, exemplary. But we'll come to that later. She calls the sequence of pictures *Trackers*, and this requires an explanation.

There are one million Palestinians today living with official papers, as underclass citizens, in the state of Israel. On their papers they are described as Israeli-Arabs. (If they publicly claim to be Palestinians, they risk a prison sentence.) Among the Israeli-Arabs are Bedouin families.

From these families a small number of men – less than one hundred a year – volunteer to join the Israeli army, where they will be trained and used as military scouts, who are known as Trackers. The trackers, who are exclusively 'Israeli-Arabs', do much of the army's dangerous field reconnaissance work. It is they who are sent ahead, whenever the Command reckons there may be resistance, to clear a terrain of land-mines, snipers, possible ambushes. The trackers are initially trained together in groups of about twenty or thirty. Once trained, they are separated out and allotted alone to units of the Israeli Defence Force, or the IDF as the army calls itself.

After three years' service, a tracker may volunteer again to become a professional soldier, whereby he will be very much better paid. The IDF Command accepts only a small number of such volunteers. The professional trackers have a professional advantage over Israeli soldiers because of their familiarity with local customs, habits and ways of calculation.

Ahlam Shibli's pictures are discreet, elusive and persistent. They contain the minimum of general information and they never report about incidents or events. One has the impression that each one has been taken just after something has happened. Not because Shibli was too slow, but because what interests her is *affect*. Events, as such, do not (at least in this project) concern her; the impact of an event on a life does. And so she is prepared to wait.

She watches the military training of the trackers, trackers going on leave, a cemetery with soldiers' graves, the taking of an oath of allegiance to the IDF sworn on the Koran, the interior of a house with family pictures on the wall, new houses being slowly built thanks to the professional army pay the trackers are earning. Each different location leads slyly to a query. For these men, what constitutes a home? Or, more slyly: To where and what do they have a sense of belonging?

There is never anybody there in the picture to tell us what happened just before it was taken. All we can do is to look at the participants who remain and then guess for ourselves and, like Shibli, wait. The effect of the whole series (eighty-five photos) is cumulative. They fit together to make a whole. Yet what does the whole add up to?

For Bedouin the issue of home and what constitutes a home is as entwined as a rope. Traditionally they are a nomadic people. Two or three generations ago, particularly in the Sinai, many Bedouin families became sedentary, yet the land they settled on belonged to somebody else, and on it they had minimal rights. A confused situation in which atavistic memories perhaps play a part. For nomads, home is not an address, home is what they carry with them.

What do the trackers carry?

Ahlam Shibli is soul-searching. Yet she avoids soulfulness

and never seeks a confession. She watches patiently from the side. One might say she was a storyteller, yet this would be to simplify her chosen role. (There are great photographic storytellers – André Kertesz, for example.) Ahlam Shibli, I would say, is a fortune-teller. She observes intensely, reads the signs, guesses and proffers her prophesy which, like a soothsayer's, is both sharp and unclear; it lays out the chances like playing cards, yet doesn't select one.

Select three. In the first, three trackers, sheltering, take a rest, and one of them is writing something on a public wall. In the second, a man asleep in the daytime has pulled a cover over his face. In the third are the photos a tracker has framed of himself as an IDF warrior, on a wall in his house, beside an old map of Palestine.

In each one, differently expressed, is the same dilemma concerning identity and whereabouts.

What are they carrying?

Traditionally, and over the centuries, nomadic Bedouin clans have offered their services to any invading force – be it Egyptian, Turkish, British – whenever they recognized that they themselves, with all their guerrilla skills, were nevertheless outflanked. They did this, however, to avoid being disbanded and in order to remain independent, unchallengeable on their own almost impenetrable territories. It was a cunning strategy for continuity which often succeeded.

Today, the circumstances for Israeli Bedouins have become

very different. They have been hounded off their land and stripped of their economic means of survival. In their own Negev desert they are treated as criminal trespassers, and their crops are sprayed with herbicide from IDF helicopters.

To grasp finally what this means we have to take account of the extremity of the Palestinian situation in general. The Palestinian–Israeli conflict has lasted nearly sixty years. The military occupation of Palestine – the longest in history – has lasted nearly forty years. Scarcely necessary to repeat all the facts that this occupation entails, for they have been internationally recognized and condemned.

What is sometimes forgotten about this continuing conflict – for the Palestinians continue to resist – is the disparity, the inequality of means, whether in terms of fire-power or defence.

Such a disparity of resources and arms recalls the mid-twentieth century colonial wars of liberation, and if we want to understand the trackers' dilemma we could not do better than consult the writings of Frantz Fanon, who was a visionary prophet of those struggles. At the end of *Black Skin, White Masks*, he writes: 'At the conclusion of this study, I want the world to recognize, with me, the open door of every consciousness.' Ahlam Shibli, writing about her *Trackers*, refers often to Frantz Fanon.

As a doctor and psychiatrist from Martinique working in Algeria, Fanon explained how colonial domination, how the disparity of means between the invader and the indige-nous, how the contempt inwritten into every encounter between the armed and the unarmed, besides producing revolt, can also lead to a gash in those allegiances which maintain a person's sense of self. And that this happens most frequently and woundingly amongst the poorest and the most underprivileged of the trampled-on.

An image may help to make this more clear. Consider the opposite syndrome, which is that of the megalomaniac. Every encounter with another person works for the megalomaniac like a held-up mirror in which he sees himself reflected and decked out in his own glory. For the colonized, who has lost his sense of self, every encounter is a mirror in which he sees nothing but a soiled djellaba. Both held-up mirrors hide the other as she or he really is. And so it happens that the colonized, in order to disassociate himself from the soiled djellaba, dreams of wearing the uniform or carrying the flag of his oppressor. Not his enemy, his oppressor.

The Bedouin are amongst the most underprivileged of Palestinians and they have lost, for the most part, their nomadic liberty and the pride that went with it. So it can happen, as Fanon foresaw, that they split themselves in two, and, tearing themselves apart, wear the mask of their oppressors. Many change their names from Ahmed to José, from Mohammed to Moshe. Yet, in doing this, the trackers do not refind their own bodies, their noble bodies that are calumnied by the false image of the soiled djellaba.

The man with the bed cover pulled over his head is dreaming of what? One can never guess at what somebody else is dreaming. *Yet he can probably not guess at his own dream.*

Something like this is what the trackers carry.

The work of Ahlam Shibli makes no direct political comment on the Israeli–Palestinian conflict; it refrains from slogans. Yet I believe that in today's global context it is politically important – or, as I said, exemplary. And I will try to explain why.

Ahlam Shibli herself comes from a Bedouin family. As a young girl she was herding goats in Galilee. Later, after studying at university, she became a photographer of international renown.

Long ago, she made the opposite existential choice to the trackers whom she shows in these photos. She believes in the justice of the Palestinian cause and has protested as a patriot and a photographer against the illegal Israeli Occupation. For her, as for most Palestinians, the trackers can be considered traitors. They have joined an army which is oppressing the Palestinian people and they stalk to kill and capture those who actively resist that army. Traitors . . . In certain circumstances, they must be treated as such.

Nevertheless Ahlam Shibli feels a need to go beyond, and search behind the simplifying label. Because she is a Bedouin herself? Maybe, but the question is naive. What counts is the result. Because she is Bedouin, she was able to search behind the label and discover what she had to discover. With these photographs she posed the question: What price are they paying for their decision to become trackers? Then she waited for the enigmatic answers which she found in her darkroom. And these she makes public.

How is this political? In the mid-twentieth century Walter Benjamin wrote: 'The state of emergency in which we live is not the exception but the rule. We must attain to a concept of history that is in keeping with this insight.'

Within such a concept of history we have to come to see that every simplification, every label, serves only the interests of those who wield power; the more extensive their power, the greater their need for simplifications. And, by contrast, the interests of those who suffer under, or struggle against this blind power, are served now and for the long, long future by the recognition and acceptance of diversity, differences and complexities.

These photographs are a contribution to such an acceptance and recognition.

I will end by quoting Frantz Fanon once more: 'No, we do not want to catch up with anyone. What we want to do is to go forward all the time, night and day, in the company of Man, in the company of all men. The caravan should not be stretched out, for in that case each line will hardly see those who precede it; and men who no longer recognize each other meet less and less together, and talk to each other less and less . . .'

2

Jitka Hanzlová

(Born in the Carpathian mountains, Czechoslovakia. 1958.)

The way I go is the way back to see the future.

Jitka Hanzlová

THE FOREST IN QUESTION is far away, near the Carpathian mountains, beside the Czech village where she lived as a child. The images could be of another forest, but not for Jitka. Over the years she has returned to hers. She goes into it alone, and if not alone does not take pictures.

Many nature photographs are like fashion photos. This is not to dismiss them; they record and admit pleasure. Mountaintops, waterfalls, meadows, lakes, beech trees in autumn, are asked to stand there, wearing themselves and giving the camera a moody look. And why not? They are reminders of the pleasure of at last arriving after hours in airports. Nature as hostess.

In Jitka's pictures there is no welcome. They have been taken from the inside. The deep inside of a forest, perceived like the inside of a glove by a hand within it.

She speaks of the between-forest. This is because, in the same valley as her village, there are two forests which join. Yet the preposition *between* belongs to forests in general. It's what they are about. A forest is what exists between its trees, between its dense undergrowth and its clearings, between all its life cycles and their different time-scales, ranging from solar energy to insects that live for a day. A forest is also a meeting place between those who enter it and something unnameable and attendant, waiting behind a tree or in the undergrowth. Something intangible and within touching distance. Neither silent nor audible. It is not only visitors who feel this attendant something; hunters and foresters who can read unwritten signs are even more keenly aware of it.

'I went to the forest-hills early in the morning when the forest awakes. Standing there I breathed in the wind, the unruffled voices of the birds and the silence which I love. And then when I was concentrating on a picture, I stopped hearing the silence around me. It was as if I was somewhere else, like in a film. The forest started to move and, as I looked through the camera, I experienced fear. Maybe it was just the framing and the stillness of the evening. As if the birds and the crickets had stopped their singing, as if the wind had come to a stop in the valley. Nothing but nothing to hear. No birds, no wind, no people, no crickets. The darkness of the light and this other silence made my hair stand on end . . . I could not exactly place the fear, but it was coming from the inside. It was the first time I felt this so intensely, but not the last. I escaped! What's the basis of this fear of mine? Why? I'm not afraid of animals or of the forest. The place is safe.'

Throughout history and prehistory forests have offered shelter, a hiding-place, whilst also being places in which a wanderer can be ultimately lost. They oblige us to recognize how much is hidden.

It's a commonplace to say that photographs interrupt or arrest the flow of time. They do it, however, in thousands of different ways. Cartier-Bresson's 'decisive moment' is different from Atget's slowing-down to a standstill, or from Thomas Struth's ceremonial stopping of time. What is strange about some of Jitka's forest photos – not her photos of other subjects – is that they appear to have stopped nothing!

In a space without gravity there is no weight, and these pictures of hers are, as it were, weightless in terms of time. It is as if they have been taken *between* times, where there is none.

What is intangible and within touching distance in a forest may be the presence of a kind of timelessness. Not the abstract timelessness of metaphysical speculation, nor the metaphorical timelessness of cyclic, seasonal repetition. Forests exist in time, they are, God knows, subject to history; and today many are catastrophically being obliterated for the quick pursuit of profit.

Yet in a forest there are 'events' which have not found their place in any of the forest's numberless time-scales, and which exist between those scales. What events? you ask.

Some are in Jitka's photographs. They are what remains unnameable in the photographs after we have made an inventory of everything that is recognizable.

The Ancient Greeks named events like these *dryads*. My lumberjack friends from Bergamo refer to the forest as a separate kingdom, a 'realm' on its own. Wilfredo Lam painted equivalent events in his imagined jungle. Yet let's be clear. We are not talking about fantasies. Jitka spoke of the forest's silence. The diametric opposite of such a silence is music. In music, every event that occurs is accommodated within the single seamless time-scale of that music. In the silence of the forest, certain events are unaccommodated and cannot be placed in time. Being like this, they both disconcert and entice the observer's imagination: for they are like another creature's experience of duration. We feel them occurring, we feel their presence, yet we cannot confront them, for they are occurring for us somewhere between past, present and future.

The philosopher Heidegger, for whom a forest was a metaphor for all reality – and the task of the philosopher was to find the *weg*, the woodcutters' path through it – spoke of 'coming into the nearness of distance' and I believe this was his way of approaching the forest phenomenon I am trying to define. Just as Jitka's formulation is another. 'The way I go is the way back to see the future.' Both reverse the hourglass.

To make sense of what I'm suggesting it is necessary to

reject the notion of time that began in Europe during the eighteenth century and is closely linked with the positivism and linear accountability of modern capitalism: the notion that a single time, which is unilinear, regular, abstract and irreversible, carries everything. All other cultures have proposed a coexistence of various times surrounded in some way by the timeless.

Return to the forests that belong to history. In Jitka's there is often a sense of waiting, yet what is it that is waiting? And is waiting the right word? A patience. A patience practised by what? A forest incident. An incident we can neither name, describe, nor place. And yet is there.

The intricacy of the crossing paths and crossing energies in a forest – the paths of birds, insects, mammals, spores, seeds, reptiles, ferns, lichens, worms, trees, etc., etc. – is unique; perhaps in certain areas on the seabed there exists a comparable intricacy, but there man is a recent intruder, whereas, with all his sense perceptions, he came from the forest. Man is the only creature who lives within at least two time-scales: the biological one of his body and the one of his consciousness. (This is perhaps what grants him his sixth sense.) Every one of the crossing energies operating in a forest has its own time-scale. From the ant to the oak tree. From the process of photosynthesis to the process of fermentation. In this intricate conglomeration of times, energies and exchanges there occur 'incidents' that are recalcitrant incidents, unaccommodated in any time-scale and therefore (temporarily?) waiting *between*. These are what Jitka photographs.

The longer one looks at Jitka Hanzlová's pictures of a forest, the clearer it becomes that a break-out from the prison of modern time is possible. The dryads beckon. You may slip between – but unaccompanied.

Notes

I Would Softly Tell My Love

[1] Nazim Hikmet, *The Moscow Symphony*. Trans., Taner Baybars. Rapp and Whiting Ltd, 1970.

[2] Ibid.

[3] Hikmet, *Prague Dawn*. Trans., Randy Blasing and Muten Konuk. Persea Books, 1994.

[4] Hikmet, *You*. Trans., Blasing and Konuk. Ibid.

[5] Trans., John Berger.

[6] Hikmet, *Letter from Poland*. Trans., John Berger.

[7] Hikmet, *9–10pm. Poems*. Trans., Blasing and Konuk.

[8] Hikmet, *On a painting by Abidine, entitled The Long March*. Trans., John Berger.

[9] Hikmet, *Under the Rain*. Trans Özen Ozüner and John Berger.

The Chorus in Our Heads or Pier Paolo Pasolini

[1] *La Rabbia*. Produced by Gastone Ferranti (OPUS Film), Galata presentation, 1963.

A Master of Pitilessness?
[1] 'Words.' Published in *SAND and Other Poems*, 1986.

Ten Dispatches About Endurance in Face of Walls
[1] Andrei Platonov, *Soul*. Trans., Robert and Elizabeth Chandler and Olga Meerson. Harvill, 2003.

[2] Ibid.

[3] Ibid.

[4] *The Portable Platonov*. Trans., Robert and Elizabeth Chandler. Glas Publishers, 1999.

[5] *Soul*. Op cit.

[6] *Soul*. Op cit.

[7] Platonov, *The Fierce and Beautiful World*. Trans., Joseph Barnes. New York Review Books, 2000.

[8] Ibid.

[9] Ibid.